The Tale of Thorlief the Earl's Poet

Original Text, Translations, and Word Lists

Translated by Matthew Leigh Embleton

Copyright ©2025 Matthew Leigh Embleton. All rights reserved.

The Tale of Thorlief the Earl's Poet

The Tale of Thorlief the Earl's Poet (*Old Norse*) 4
Word List *(Old Norse to English)* 26
Word List *(English to Old Norse)* 41
The Tale of Thorlief the Earl's Poet (*Old Icelandic*) 54
Word List *(Old Icelandic to English)* 76
Word List *(English to Old Icelandic)* 91
A Word Comparison of Old Norse and Old Icelandic Words 104

Cover: Old Norse text over an outline of Iceland. Author's design.

The original Old Norse and Old Icelandic texts are in the public domain.
These translations ©2022 Matthew Leigh Embleton
©2025 Matthew Leigh Embleton (This Edition)

Acknowledgments

I have long been fascinated by languages and history, and I am very grateful to the special people in my life who have supported and encouraged me in my work. Thank you for believing in me. You know who you are.

Introduction

Old Norse is a North Germanic language spoken by inhabitants of Scandinavia from about the 7th to the 15th centuries. Old Icelandic is a variety of Old West Norse that emerged during the Norse settlement of Iceland in the second half of the 9th century. The rich tradition of Icelandic literature survived by oral tradition over several centuries before being written down in the 13th Century. The Tale of Thorlief the Earl's Poet (*Þorleifs þáttr jarlsskálds*) is one of the many Tales of Icelanders or *Íslendingaþættir*. The word '*þáttr*' (plural: '*þættir*') translates as a strand of rope or a yarn, comparable to the word 'yarn' in English sometimes used to refer to a story.

This book contains:
- The Tale of Thorlief the Earl's Poet (*Þorleifs þáttr jarlsskálds*) (Old Norse Version)
- An Old Norse to English Word List
- An English to Old Norse Word List
- The Tale of Thorlief the Earl's Poet (*Þorleifs þáttr jarlsskálds*) (Old Icelandic Version)
- An Old Icelandic to English Word List
- An English to Old Icelandic Word List
- A Word Comparison of Old Norse and Old Icelandic words

The texts are presented in their original form, with a literal word-for-word line-by-line translation, and a Modern English translation, all side-by-side. In this way, it is possible to see and feel how the worked and how it has evolved. This book is designed to be of use and interest to anyone with a passion for the Old Norse or Old Icelandic language, Norse history, or languages and history in general.

The Tale of Thorlief the Earl's Poet (*Old Norse*)

Old Norse	Literal	English
1	**1**	**1**
Nú skal segja þann œvintýr er gerðist á ofanverðum dögum Hákonar Hlaðajarls, í hverjum kynstrum, göldrum og gerningum hann varð forsmáðr og mjǫk at verðugu, því at hans mannillska og guðníðingskapr varð mörgum manni til mikils þunga og óbœtilegs skaða andar og líkama.	Now shall say then adventure that happened in the-uppermost days Hakon Earl-Of-Lade, about who's strange, magical-arts and witchcraft he was shamed and much to honour, because that he man-evil and idol-worship became many people to much heavy and un-redeemable damage soul and body.	Now shall be told the adventure that happened in the early days of Hakon the earl of Lade, about his strange magic and witchcraft which greatly shamed his honour, because this evil man and his idolatry became a heavy burden to many people, and caused irreparable harm to soul and body.
Varð honum þat sem margan tímir at þá er hegningartíminn er kominn er eigi hœgt undan at komast því at þat er óvinarins náttúra at þann manninn sem hann þykist fullkomið vald á eiga og önga von á til guðs blekkir hann fyrst og blygðar með krókóttum kyndugskap sinna bölvaðra slœgða í framleiðslu hans ljótu lífsdaga en at þrotnum hans stundlegum lífstíma verðr hann drekktr í dökkri dýflissu dálegra kvala með eymd og ánauð utan enda.	Became to-him that as many time that then was punishment-time was came that not possible out-of to come because that it was the-enemy's nature that then people which he thought full-coming power that not and none hope of to God deceived he first and shame with devious cunning his cursed slyness in causing his ghastly life-days then that waning his temporary lifetime became he drowned in dark dungeon harmful torment with misery and enslavement without end.	It befell him, as it does to many, when the time of punishment came, he could not come out of it, as it was the devil's nature to deceive people who he thinks he has full power over, and who has no hope of God's mercy. First comes shame with devious cunning and cursed slyness, causing a ghastly life, and in the waning of his temporary life, he is drowned in the dark dungeon of harmful torment, with misery and enslavement without end.
2	**2**	**2**
Þá bjó Ásgeir rauðfeldr á Brekku í Svarfaðardal.	Then lived Asgeir Red-Cloak at Brekka in Svarfardal.	Then Asgeir Red-Cloak lived at Brekka in Svafardal.
Hann var ríkr maðr og stórœttaðr.	He was powerful man and great-family.	He was a powerful man from a great family.
Þórhildr hét kona hans.	Thorhild named wife his.	His wife was named Thorhild.
Hún var vitr kona og vinsœl og skörungr mikill.	She was wise woman and popular and noble much.	She was a very wise, popular, and noble woman.

The Tale of Thorlief the Earl's Poet (Old Norse)

Old Norse	Literal	English
Þau áttu þrjá syni og voru allir efnilegir.	They had three sons and were all promising.	They had three sons, all of whom were promising.
Ólafr hét son þeirra hinn elsti og var kallaðr völubrjótr, annar Helgi hinn frœkni og koma þeir báðir meir við aðrar sögr en þessa.	Olaf named son theirs the eldest and was called knuckle-breaker, another Helgi the brave and came they both more with other sagas than this.	Their eldest son was named Olaf, who was called 'knuckle-breaker', the second son was called Helgi the brave, and they appear in other sagas than this one.
Þorleifr hét hinn yngsti son þeirra.	Thorleif named the youngest son theirs.	Their youngest son was named Thorleif.
Hann var snemma gildr og gervilegr og hinn mesti atgervimaðr um íþróttir.	He was early-age capable and talented and the most accomplished-man at skilled.	He was fully capable at an early age, an accomplished man and skilful.
Hann var skáld gott.	He was a-poet good.	He was a good poet
Hann var á fóstri með Miðfjarðar-Skeggja móðrbróðr sínum at Reykjum í Miðfirði þar til er hann var átján vetra gamall.	He was in fostered with Midfjorder-Skeggi mother's-brother his at Reykir in Midfjord there until that he was eighteen winters old.	He was brought up with his uncle Midfjorder-Skeggi at Reykir in Midfjord there until he was eighteen years old.
Skeggi unni mikið Þorleifi og lagði við hann ástfóstr.	Skeggi loved much Thorleif and had with him foster-care.	Skeggi loved Thorleif very much and brought him up with care.
Þat töluðu menn at Skeggi mundi fleira kenna Þorleifi í frœðum fornlegum en aðrir mundu vita.	This told people that Skeggi would more teach Thorleif in instruction ancient-ways than others would know.	People said that Skeggi would teach Thorleif more about the ways of magic than others would know.
Þá fór Þorleifr heim til föðr síns.	Then went Thorleif home to father his.	Then Thorleif went home to his father.
Hann vó Klaufa böggva með fulltingi Ólafs bróðr síns en til eftirmáls eftir Klaufa var Karl hinn rauði og gekk svo fast at at Þorleifr varð útlœgr og ger í burt úr Svarfaðardal.	He killed Klaufi the-mauler with assistance Olaf's brother his and to after-the-case after Klaufi was Karl the Red and went so closed it that Thorleif became outlaw and made to away from-out-of Svarfardal.	He killed Klaufi the mauler with the help of his brother Olaf, and in the following legal case was Karl the Red, and so it concluded that Thorleif became an outlaw and banished from Svafardal.
Ljótólfr goði hafði fylgt Yngvildi fagurkinn systr Þorleifs.	Ljotolf chieftain had followed Yngvild Fair-Cheek sister Thorleif's.	Ljotolf the chieftain lived with Yngvild the fair-cheek, Thorleif's sister.

The Tale of Thorlief the Earl's Poet (Old Norse)

Old Norse	Literal	English
Hann kom Þorleifi í skip á Gáseyri.	He came Thorleif to ship at Gaseyri.	He brought Thorleif to a ship at Gaseyri.
Þorleifr varð afturreka.	Thorleif became back-driven.	But Thorleif was driven back.
Hann var um veturinn á laun ýmist með Ljótólfi goða eða Ásgeiri föðr sínum.	He was about winter in secrecy either with Ljotolf the-chieftain or Asgeir father his.	During the winter he was hiding with Ljotolf the chieftain or his father Asgeir.
Nam hann þá at föðr sínum marga fornfrœði því at hann var sagðr margkunnandi.	Took he then to father his many ancient-ways because that he was said many-known.	He then took to learning many of the ancient ways, as it is said that he knew many things.
Var þá Þorleifr nítján vetra.	Was then Thorleif nineteen winters.	Thorleif was then nineteen winters old.
Karl leitaði fast eftir um Þorleif og urðu þar um veturinn margir atburðir, þeir er frásagnar eru verðir sem segir í Svarfdœla sögu.	Karl sought closely after about Thorleif and became there about winter many events, they are from-told are will-be as said in Svarfardal saga.	Karl looked closely for Thorleif, and from there came many events, which are told in Svafardal Saga.
Um vorið eftir fór Þorleifr vestr til Skeggja fóstra síns og frænda og biðr hann ásjá og umráða með sér um þessi mál.	About spring after travelled Thorleif west to Skeggi foster-father his and kinsmen and asked him assistance and about-advice with him about this matter.	About the following spring, Thorleif travelled west to Skeggi his foster father and kinsman, and asked for his help and guidance in this matter.
Og með styrk og ráðum Miðfjarðar-Skeggja og Ljótólfs goða fer Þorleifr og kaupir sér skip at kaupmönnum er uppi stóð í Blönduósi og rœðr háseta til og fór síðan heim á Brekku og hitti föðr sinn og móðr og beiddist af þeim fararefna og fékk svo mikinn fjárhlut sem honum þótti sér þarfa og at vordögum lét hann varning sinn til skips binda og fór í brott af Brekku alfari og bat vel fyrir föðr sínum og móðr og Miðfjarðar-Skeggja fóstra sínum.	And with support and advice Midfjorder-Skeggi and Ljotolf the-chieftain went Thorleif and bought himself a-ship from trading-men that up stood in Blonduos and hired first-mate for and travelled afterwards home to Brekka and met father his and mother and asked of them travel-goods and got so much fee-lot as he thought he-himself needed and to spring-days had he wares his to ship bound and travelled to away from Brekka for-good and bid well for father his and mother and Midfjorder-Skeggi foster-father his.	And with the support and advice of Midfjorder-Skeggi and Ljotolf the chieftain, Thorleif went and bought himself a ship from merchants up in Blonduos, and hired a first mate for it. After that he then travelled home to Brekka and met his father and mother, asking for wares and travel goods, and he got as much money as he thought he needed. In the first days of spring he brought his wares to his ship, bound them up, and travelled away from Brekka once and for all, wishing his father and mother well, and Midfjorder-Skeggi, his foster father.

The Tale of Thorlief the Earl's Poet (Old Norse)

Old Norse	Literal	English
# 3	# 3	# 3
Nú lætr Þorleifr í haf og byrjar honum vel og kemr skipi sínu í Vík austr.	Now left Thorleif to sea and fair-wind he-had well and came ship his into Vik east.	Now Thorleif set out to sea and got a fair wind, and his ship came to Vik in the east.
Hákon Hlaðajarl var þá í Víkinni.	Hakon Earl-Of-Lade was then in The-bay.	Hakon was the earl of Lade at Vik.
Þorleifr gekk á land og lét ryðja skip sitt.	Thorleif went to the-land and had cleared ship his.	Thorleif went to land and had is ship unloaded.
Hann hitti jarlinn og kvaddi hann.	He met the-earl and greeted him.	He met the earl and greeted him.
Jarl tók honum vel og spurði hann at nafni, ætt og kynferði en Þorleifr sagði honum.	The-earl received him well and asked him of name, ancestors and kinsmen-origins and Thorleif told him.	The earl received him well and asked his name, ancestry, and origins, and Thorleif told him.
Jarl spurði og margra tíðinda af Íslandi en Þorleifr sagði honum ofléttlega.	The-earl asked of much news of Iceland and Thorleif told him willingly.	The earl asked for much news of Iceland, and Thorleif told him.
Þá sagði jarl:	Then said the-earl:	Then the earl said:
"Svo er orðið Þorleifr at vér viljum hafa sölr af þér og hásetum þínum".	"So has become Thorleif that we wish-to have sale of you and crew yours".	"So it is, Thorleif, that we wish to buy some things from you and your crew".
Þorleifr svarar:	Thorleif answered:	Thorleif answered:
"Vér höfum lítinn varninginn herra en oss eru þó aðrir kaupunautar hentugri og munuð þér láta oss sjálfráða vera at selja þeim góss vort og peninga sem oss líkar".	"We have little wares lord and us we-are though other customers more-convenient and shall you allow us ourselves-decide being for to-sell them belongings ours and money as we like".	"We have little in the way of wares, my lord, and we need more useful customers, and you shall allow us to decide for ourselves who to sell our belongings to as we like".
Jarli þótti hann þykklega svara og mislíkaði orð hans mjök og skildu við svo búið.	Earl thought he arrogantly answered and misliked words his much and parted with so settled.	The earl thought he had answered arrogantly, and disliked his words, and with that they parted.

The Tale of Thorlief the Earl's Poet (Old Norse)

Old Norse	Literal	English
Þorleifr fór nú til manna sinna og svaf af um nóttina og um morguninn rís hann upp og fer í kaupstaðinn og fréttist fyrir um góða kaupunauta og kaupslagar við þá um daginn.	Thorleif travelled now to men his and slept of about the-night and about morning rose he up and travelled to market-town and sought for about food customers and bargaining with then about the-day.	Thorleif went back to his men and slept through the night, and in the morning he got up and travelled to town and sought good customers, and bargained with them throughout the day.
Og er jarl spurði þat fór hann með fjölmenni til skips Þorleifs og lét taka þar menn alla og binda.	And when the-earl learned that travelled he with following-men to ships Thorleif's and had took there men all and tied-up.	And when the earl learned of this, he travelled with his followers to Thorleif's ship and took all the men and had them tied up.
Síðan rændi hann þar fjárhlut öllum og kastaði á sinni eign en lét brenna skipið at köldum kolum.	Afterwards robbed he there financial-share of-all and cast about himself owning and had burnt the-ship to cold coals.	Afterwards he robbed them of all their wealth and took it for himself, and had the ship burnt to coals.
Og eftir þetta lét hann skjóta ásum milli búðanna og lét þar hengja við alla förunauta Þorleifs.	And after this had he launched poles between booths and had them hanged with all companions Thorleif's.	After this he had poles raised between booths and had all of Thorleif's companions hanged.
Síðan fór jarl í brott og hans menn og tók at sér varning þann er Þorleifr hafði átt og skipti upp með sínum mönnum.	Afterwards travelled the-earl to away and his men and took then for-himself wares then that Thorleif had had and exchanged up with his men.	Afterwards the earl went away with his men, taking all the wares and dividing it among his men.
En um kveldið er Þorleifr kom heim og œtlaði at vitja manna sinna sem hann gerði sá hann vegsummerki hversu við hans félaga hafði farið verið og þóttist vita at Hákon jarl mundi þessu vonda verki valdið hafa og spyr nú eftir þessum tíðindum glögglega.	Then about evening when Thorleif came home and intended to know men his what he had-done saw he traces how-so with his companions had gone been and thought certainly that Hakon earl would this wicked work caused had and learned now after this news clearly.	In the evening when Thorleif came home and looked for his men as usual, he saw traces of what had happened with his companions, and thought certainly that Earl Hakon caused this evil deed, and afterwards he learned the full news clearly.
Og er hann hafði þessi tíðindi sannlega spurt þá kvat hann vísu:	And when he had this news truly learned then spoke he this-verse:	And when he learned the news, then he spoke this verse:
Hrollir hugr minn illa. Hefir drengr skaða fengið sé eg á sléttri eyri, svarri, báts og knarrar.	Shivering heart mine badly. Have men damage caught see i this levelled sand, grave, boats and merchant-ships.	My heart shivers badly. Men have caught damage, I see this levelled sand, grave, both ship and boat.

The Tale of Thorlief the Earl's Poet (Old Norse)

Old Norse	Literal	English
Hinn er upp réð brenna öldu fíl fyrir skaldi, hver veit nema kol knarrar köld fýsi mig gjalda.	Those are up ruled burned wave elephant before the-poet, who knows except the-coals of-the-ship cold desire shall-i repay.	Those that ruled to burn the elephant of the waves, who knows except the coals of the ship cold desire I to repay.

4

Svo er sagt at eftir þenna atburð kom Þorleifr sér í skip með kaupmönnum og sigldu suðr til Danmerkr og fór hann á fund Sveins konungs og var með honum um veturinn.	So it-is said that after those events came Thorleif himself in a-ship with trading-men and sailed south to Denmark and travelled he to meet Svein the-king and was with him about winter.	It is said that after this Thorleif went on a ship with trading-men and sailed south to Denmark, and he travelled to meet king Svein and stayed with him over the winter.
En er hann hafði þar eigi lengi verið var þat einn dag at Þorleifr gekk fyrir konung og beiddi hann hlýða kvæði því er hann hafði ort um hann.	Then when he had there not long been was it one day that Thorleif went before the-king and asked him to-hear poem since that he had worded about him.	Then when he had not long been there, one day Thorleif went before the king and asked hi to hear a poem that he had composed about him.
Konungr spurði hvort hann væri skáld.	The-king asked whether he was a-poet.	The king asked whether he was a poet.
Þorleifr svarar:	Thorleif answered:	Thorleif answered:
"Þat er eftir því sem þér viljið dœmt hafa herra er þér heyrið".	"It is after therefore which to-you will deem have lord when you hear".	"That is for you to judge, lord, when you have heard it".
Konungr bat hann þá fram flytja.	The-king asked him then from to-carry.	The king then asked him to perform.
Þorleifr kvat þá fertuga drápu og er þetta stef í:	Thorleif spoke then forty phrases and is this stave in:	Thorleif spoke forty verses and among them is this stave:
Oft með œrnri giftu öðlings himins röðla Jóta gramr hinn ítri Englandi roðið branda.	Often with merry luck noble heaven's wheel Jutland warrior the high-born England reddened swords.	Often with merry luck from noble heaven's wheel the high-born Jutland warrior reddened swords in England.
Konungr lofaði mjök kvæðið og allir þeir er heyrðu og sögðu bæði vel kveðið og skörulega fram flutt.	The-king praised much the-poem and all they who heard and said both well spoken and boldly forward performed.	The king praised the poem very much, and all those who heard it said it was both well spoken and boldly performed.

The Tale of Thorlief the Earl's Poet (Old Norse)

Old Norse	Literal	English
Konungr gaf Þorleifi at kvœðislaunum hring þann er stóð mörk og þat sverð er til kom hálf mörk gulls og bat hann lengi með sér vera.	The-king gave Thorleif to poem's-reward a-ring then was stood a-mark and with a-sword was to come half a-mark of-gold and invited him long with him to-be.	The king gave Thorleif a reward for the poem, a ring that was worth a mark of gold, and a sword worth half a mark of gold, and he invited him to stay with him.
Þorleifr gekk til sœtis og þakkaði vel konungi.	Thorleif went to sit and thanked well the-king.	Thorleif took his place and thanked the king well.
Og leið svo fram nokkura hríð og ekki lengi áðr en Þorleifr ógladdist svo mjǫk at hann gáði varla undir drykkjuborð at ganga eða samsœtis við sína bekkjunauta.	And passed so from some awhile and not long before that Thorleif un-gladdened so much that he cared scarcely up-to drinking-tables and went either banquet with himself bench-fellows.	And so it passed, and it was not long before Thorleif became so unhappy that he scarcely cared to go to the drinking tables to feast or talk with his bench mates.
Finnr konungr þetta bráðlega og lætr kalla Þorleif fyrir sig og mælti:	Found the-king this quickly and had called Thorleif before him and spoke:	The king soon noticed this and had Thorleif called before him, and asked:
"Hvat veldr ógleði þinni er þú gáir varla at halda háttum við oss?"	"What brought-about un-gladness yours that you care scarcely to hold custom with us?"	"What has brought about your unhappiness, that you hardly keep to our customs?"
Þorleifr svarar:	Thorleif answered:	Thorleif answered:
"Þat munuð þér heyrt hafa herra at sá er skyldr at leysa annars vandrœði er at spyr".	"That should you heard have lord that so who should to solve another's difficulty who that asks".	"You must have heard, lord, that he who asks another's difficulty should solve it for him".
"Segðu fyrst",	"Say-you first",	"Tell it first",
segir konungr.	said the-king.	said the king.
Þorleifr svarar:	Thorleif answered:	Thorleif answered:
"Eg hefi kveðið vísr nokkurar í vetr er eg kalla Konrvísr er eg hefi ort um Hákon jarl því at jarl er kona kenndr í skáldskap.	"If have poem verses some in winter that i call Woman-Verses that i have worded about Hakon earl because that the-earl is a-woman known in poetry.	"I have composed some verses in the winter, that I call Women Verses, that I composed about Earl Hakon, because the earl is called a woman in poetry.

The Tale of Thorlief the Earl's Poet (Old Norse)

Old Norse	Literal	English
Nú ógleðr mig þat herra ef eg fœ eigi orlof af yðr at fara til Noregs og fœra jarli kvœðið".	Now un-glad me that lord if i get not leave of yours to travel to Norway and bring the-earl the-poem".	I will be unhappy, lord, if I do not get your leave to travel to Norway to bring the earl the poem".
"Þú skalt at vísu fá orlof",	"You shall this certainly get leave",	"You shall certainly have leave",
segir konungr, "og skaltu þó heita oss áðr at koma aftr til vor þat fljótasta sem þú getr því at vér viljum þín ekki missa sakir íþrótta þinna".	said the-king, "and shall-you though promise us return to come after to spring the soonest as you get therefore that we wish your not miss sake skills yours".	said the king, "and you shall promise to return to us soon after spring, because we do not wish to miss your skills".
Þorleifr hét því og fékk sér nú farning og fór norðr í Noreg og linnir eigi fyrr en hann kemr í Þrándheim.	Thorleif promised accordingly and got himself now passage and travelled north to Norway and stopped not before that he came to Trondheim.	Thorleif promised accordingly and now got himself passage to travel north to Norway, and did not stop until he came to Trondheim.
Þá sat Hákon jarl á Hlöðum.	Then sat Hakon earl at Lade.	Then Hakon sat in residence at Lade.
Þorleifr býr sér nú stafkarls gervi og bindr sér geitarskegg og tók sér eina stóra hít og lét koma undir stafkarls gervina og bjó svo um at öllum skyldi sýnast sem hann œti þann kost er hann kastaði í hítina því at gíman hennar var uppi við munn honum undir geitarskegginu.	Thorleif prepared himself now as-a-beggar character and bound himself goat-beard and took himself a large bag and had come-with under beggar's disguise and prepared so about that all should appear as he had then food that he cast in the-bag because that opening its was up by mouth his under goat-beard.	Thorleif now disguised himself as a beggar and wore a goat's beard, he also took a large bag which he kept under the disguise, and it was prepared so that everyone would think that he ate the food that he put into the bag, because the opening was up by his mouth under the goat's beard.
Síðan tekr hann hœkjr tvœr og var broddr niðr úr hvorri, fer nú þar til er hann kemr á Hlaðir.	Afterwards took he crutches two and were spikes down out-of each, travelled now there until that he came to Lade.	Afterwards he also took two crutches with spikes on the ends, and travelled until he came to Lade.
Þat var aðfangskveld jóla í þann tíma er jarl var kominn í sœti og mart stórmenni er jarl hafði at sér boðið til jólaveislunnar.	It was midwinter-evening Yule at that time when the-earl was coming to sit and many great-men that the-earl had that he invited to yule-feast.	It was the midwinter evening of Yule, when the earl was coming to sit, and there were many great men that the earl had invited to the Yule feast.

The Tale of Thorlief the Earl's Poet (Old Norse)

Old Norse	Literal	English
Karl gengr greiðlega inn í höllina en er hann kemr inn stumrar hann geysimjǫk og fellr fast á hœkjurnar og snýr til annarra stafkarla og sest niðr utarlega í hálminn.	The-old-man went quickly in to the-hall and when he came in stumbled he exceedingly-much and fell close had the-crutches and turned to other beggars and sat down out-lying of the-straw.	The old man went quickly into the hall, and when he came in, he stumbled and fell heavily on his crutches, then turned to the other beggars and sat down at the edge of the straw.
Hann var nokkuð bœginn við stafkarla og heldr harðleikinn en þeir þoldu illa er hann lét ganga á þeim stafina.	He was somewhat troubled with beggars and rather rough and they endured badly that he let go to them sticks.	He was irritable with the beggars and quite rough, and they were not happy with being knocked by his sticks.
Hrukku þeir undan og varð af þessu hark og háreysti svo at heyrði um alla höllina.	Drew they back and became of this noise and commotion so that heard about all the-hall.	They drew back and this caused noise and commotion so that all who were in the hall heard.
En er jarl verðr þessa var spyr hann hvat valdi óhljóði þessu.	Then when the-earl became this was asked he what controlled unsoundly this.	Then when the earl was aware of this, he asked what caused this din.
Honum er sagt at stafkarl einn sé sá þar kominn at svo sé illr og úrigr at ekki láti ógert.	He was said that beggar one himself saw there coming that so being bad and unruly that not had undone.	He was told that a beggar had been seen who was so bad and unruly that he stopped at nothing.
Jarl bat kalla hann fyrir sig og svo var og gert.	Earl asked call-to him before him him and so was and done.	The earl asked him to be called before him, and so it was done.
En er karl kom fyrir jarl hafði hann mjǫk stutt um kvaðningar.	And when the-old-man came before the-earl had he much short about greeting.	And when the old man came before the earl, he greeted him shortly.
Jarl spurði hann at nafni, œtt og óðali.	Earl asked him of name, ancestry and estate.	The earl asked him his name, his ancestry, and his estate.
"Óvant er nafn mitt herra at eg heiti Níðungr Gjallandason og kynjaðr úr Syrgisdölum af Svíþjóð hinni köldu.	"Not-lacking is name mine lord that i named Nidung Son-of-gjallandi and descended from Syrgsdalir in Sweden the cold.	"Not lacking is my name, lord, for I am named Nidung son of Gjallandi and descended from Syrgsdalir in Sweden the cold.
Er eg kallaðr Níðungr hinn nákvœmi.	Am i called Nidung the pernickety.	I am called Nidung the pernickety.
Hefi eg víða farið og marga höfðingja heim sótt.	Have i widely travelled and many chieftains' homes sought.	I have travelled widely and sought many chieftains' homes.

The Tale of Thorlief the Earl's Poet (Old Norse)

Old Norse	Literal	English
Gerist eg nú gamall mjǫk svo at trautt má eg aldr minn segja sakir elli og óminnis.	Becoming i now old much so that scarcely may i age mine say with-conviction age of amnesia.	I am now becoming so old that scarcely may I say my age with conviction because of amnesia.
Hefi eg mikla spurn af höfðingskap yðrum og harðfengi, visku og vinsældum, lagasetning og lítillæti, örleik og allri atgervi".	Have i much learned of lordship yours and toughness, wisdom and popularity, legislation and humility, generosity and all deeds".	I have learned much of your lordship and toughness, wisdom and popularity, legislation and humility, and your generosity in all deeds".
"Hví ertu svo harðúðigr og illr viðskiptis frá því sem aðrir stafkarlar?"	"Why are-you so harsher and ill behaved from therefore as other beggars?"	"Why are you so much harsher and badly behaved than the other beggars?"
Hann svarar:	He answered:	He answered:
"Hvat er örvænt um þann sem alls gengr andvana nema víls og vesaldar og ekki hefir þat er þarf og lengi legið úti á mörkum og skógum þó at sá verði æfr við ellina og allt saman en vanr áðr sæmd og sællífi af hinum dýrstum höfðingjum en vera nú hataðr af hverjum þorpara lítils verðum".	"What is desperation about than as all going destitution taken advantage and wretchedness and not having that which needed and long laying out in marshes and forests though that so become angry with age and all together that experienced before honour and blessed-life of other dearest chieftains but becoming now hated of each peasant little worth".	"What is desperation about other than always going in destitution, taken advantage of by wretchedness, not having what is needed, laying for a long time in the marshes and forests, though becoming so angry with age, when altogether before having experienced a blessed life of the dearest chieftains, but becoming now hated by every peasant of little worth".
Jarl mælti:	The-earl spoke:	The earl spoke:
"Ertu nokkr íþróttamaðr karl er þú segist þó með höfðingjum verið hafa?"	"Are-you anything excellent-man old-man that you say though with chieftains became have?"	"Are you excellent at anything, old man, as you say you have been with chieftains?"
Karl svarar þat megi vera þó at nokkuð hafi til þess haft verið	The-old-man answered that may be though that somewhat have until this have been	The old man answered that it may be something like that:
"þá er eg var á ungum aldri.	"then when i was of young age.	"then when I was young in age.
Komi at því sem mælt er, at hverjum karli kemr at örverpi.	Comes to therefore as said is, to each man comes to decrepitude.	But it comes, as they say, decrepitude to each and every man.

The Tale of Thorlief the Earl's Poet (Old Norse)

Old Norse	Literal	English
Er þat og talat at seigt er svöngum at skruma.	Is that also told that tough from hunger to swagger.	It is also said that it is difficult to swagger when hungry.
Mun eg og ekki við yðr skruma herra nema þér látið gefa mér at eta því at svo dregr at mér af elli, svengd og þorsta at víst eigi fæ eg staðið uppi lengr.	Should i also not with you show-off lord unless you let give me to eat because that so drawn that i-am of age, hungry and thirsty and know not can i stand up for-long.	I can't show off to you, lord, unless you give me something to eat, because I am so drawn and with age, hungry and thirsty, and I do not know how long I can stand up for.
Er slíkt harðla óhöfðinglegt at spyrja ókunna menn í hvern heim en hugsa eigi hvat mönnum hentar því at allir eru með því eðli skapaðir at bæði þurfa át og drykkju".	It-is such hardly chieftain-like to ask unknown people into one's home but think not what peoples' requirements because that all are with therefore nature shaped that both need eat and drink".	It us hardly chieftain-like to ask strangers into one's home but not think about his requirements, because we are all shaped by nature to need both food and drink".
Jarl skipaði at honum skyldi gefa kost sæmilega sem honum þarfaði.	The-earl arranged that he should give food properly as he needed.	The earl arranged that he should be given food properly as he needed.
Var og svo gert.	Was also so done.	This was done.
En er karl kom undir borð tekr hann greiðlega til matar og ryðr diska þá alla er næstir honum voru og hann náði til svo at þjónustumenn urðu at sækja kost í annan tíma.	Then the old-man came up-to the-tables took he promptly to food and cleared plates then all that nearest him were and he caught to so the servants became to sake provide for a-second time.	Then the old man came up to the tables, and he promptly took the food and cleared all the plates that were nearest to him, forcing the servants to provide a second helping.
Tók karl nú öngu ófreklegar til matar en fyrr.	Took the-old-man now not un-eagerly to food then before.	The old man was not just as eager as before.
Sýndist öllum sem hann æti en hann kastaði reyndar í hítina þá er fyrr var getið.	Seemed-to all that he ate but he cast actually in the-bag then as before was told-of.	It seemed to everyone that he ate, but the food was actually in the bag, as was told before.
Hlógu menn nú fast at karli þessum.	Laughed people now closely at the-old-man this.	People focused on the old man, and laughed.
Þjónustumenn töluðu at bæði væri at hann væri mikill og miðdigr enda gæti hann mikið etið.	Servants told that both were that he was great and broad-waist and got he much to-eat.	The servants said that he was both tall, and with a broad waist, and he could eat a lot.
Karl gaf sér ekki at því og gerði sem áðr.	The-old-man gave himself not that then and did as before.	The old man did not react, and did as before.

The Tale of Thorlief the Earl's Poet (Old Norse)

Old Norse	Literal	English

5   5   5

En er ofan voru drykkjuborð gekk Níðungr karl fyrir jarl og mælti:	When that over were drinking-tables went Nidung the-old-man before the-earl and spoke:	When the drinking tables were removed, the old man Nidung went to the earl and spoke:
"Hafið þér nú þökk fyrir herra en þó eigið þér illa þjónustumenn er allt gera verr en þér segið fyrir.	"Have you now thanks for lord but though own you bad servants that all done worst than you said before.	"You have now my thanks, lord, but you have bad servants that did everything worse than you ordered.
En nú vildi eg at þér sýnduð mér lítillæti herra og hlýdduð kvæði því er eg hefi ort um yðr".	But now wish i that to-you give-performance me a-little lord and listen-to poem because that i have worded about you".	But now I wish to give you a performance of my poem that I have composed about you".
Jarl mælti:	The-earl spoke:	The earl spoke:
"Hefir þú nokkuð fyrr kvæði ort um höfðingja?"	"Have you any before poems worded about chieftains?"	"Have you composed any poems about chieftains before?"
"Satt er þat herra",	"True is that lord",	"That is true, lord",
kvat hann.	said he.	he said.
Jarl mælti:	The-earl spoke:	The earl spoke:
"Búið þar komi at gömlum orðskvið, at þat er oft gott er gamlir kveða, og flyttu fram kvæðið karl en vér munum til hlýða".	"Done there comes that old proverb, that it is often good what old-man recites, and move forward poem old-man and we shall to listen".	"Done there is the proverb, that it is often good what an old man recites, so come forward with the poem, old man, and we shall listen".
Þá hefr karl upp kvæðið og kveðr framan til miðs og þykir jarli lof í hverri vísu og finnr at þar er getið og í framaverka Eiríks sonar hans.	Then had the-old-man upped the-poem and said in-front-of the middle and thought the-earl praise in each verse and found that there was told-of and in previous-deeds Erik's son his.	Then the old man began the poem and recited it to the middle, and the earl thought that he heard praise in each verse, and found that there were tales told about his son Erik.

The Tale of Thorlief the Earl's Poet (Old Norse)

Old Norse	Literal	English
En er á leið kvæðið þá bregðr jarli nokkuð undarlega við at óværi og kláði hleypr svo mikill um allan búkinn á honum og einna mest um þjóin at hann mátti hvergi kyrr þola og svo mikil býsn fylgdi þessum óværa at hann lét hrífa sér með kömbum þar sem þeim kom at.	But as it passed the-poem then tricked the-earl something strange from a restlessness and itching ran so much about all body of him and only most about thighs that he may each sit-still endure and so much strangeness followed this restlessness that he had scratched himself with combs there as they came to.	But as the poem continued, the earl was tricked into feeling a strange restlessness and an itching that ran all over his body, especially around his thighs so that he could hardly sit still, this uneasiness was so strange that he had scratched himself with combs wherever he could.
En þar sem þeim kom eigi at lét hann taka strigadúk og ríða á þrjá knúta og draga tvo menn milli þjóanna á sér.	Then there as they could not that had he taken sack-cloth and rose in three knots and drew two men between thighs for him.	Where he could not reach, he took a sack cloth and made three knots in it, and two men dragged it between his thighs for him.
Nú tók jarli illa at geðjast kvæðið og mælti:	Now took the-earl ill that liking the-poem and spoke:	Now the earl took badly to the poem and spoke:
"Kann þinn heljarkarl ekki betr at kveða því at mér þykir þetta eigi síðr heita mega níð en lof og lát þú um batna ella tekr þú gjöld fyrir".	"Can you hellish-old-man not better to say because that to-me seems this not less call may abuse than praise and let you about better or take you repayment for".	"Can you not recite something better you hellish old man, because it seems to me more like abuse than praise, and make it better or you will be repaid for it".
Karl hét góðu um og hóf þá upp vísr og heita Þokuvísr og standa í miðju Jarlsníði og er þetta upphaf at:	The-old-man promised improvement about and began then up verses and named Fog-verses and stood in middle-of The-earl's-abuse and was this beginning this:	The old man promised improvement and then began verses named Fog Verses, which are in the middle of the Earl's Abuse, and the beginning was this:
Þoku dregr upp hið ytra, él festist hið vestra, mökkr mun náms, af nökkvi, naðrbings kominn hingat.	Fog draws up then outside, blizzard grips the west, thick-clouds shall take, of the-ship, dragon comes here.	Fog draws up then outside, a blizzard grips the west, thick clouds shall take, of the ship, the dragon comes here.
En er hann hafði úti Þokuvísr þá var myrkt í höllinni.	When that he had finished Fog-verses then was dark in the-hall.	When he had finished the Fog Verses, it was dark in the hall.
Og er myrkt er orðið í höllinni tekr hann aftr til Jarlsníðs.	And was dark was become in the-hall took he returning to Earl's-abuse.	And when it became dark in the hall, he began the Earl Abuse verses again.

The Tale of Thorlief the Earl's Poet (Old Norse)

Old Norse	Literal	English
Og er hann kvat hinn efsta og síðasta þriðjung þá var hvert járn á gangi þat er í var höllinni án manna völdum og varð þat margra manna bani.	And as he spoke the upper and last third then was each iron-weapon from moved it that in was the-hall without man's doing and became that many people dead.	And has he recited the third and last part, then each iron weapon that as in the hall moved without man's doing, and many men became dead.
Jarl féll þá í óvit en karl hvarf þá í brott at luktum dyrum og óloknum lásum.	The-earl fell then into unconsciousness but the-old-man disappeared then to away that shut doors and undone locks.	The earl then fell into unconsciousness, but the old man disappeared away through shut doors and undone locks.
En eftir afliðið kvæðið minnkaði myrkrið og gerði bjart í höllinni.	Then after following the-poem decreased the-darkness and it-was bright in the-hall.	Then following after the poem the darkness decreased, and it was bright again in the hall.
Jarl raknaði við og fann at honum hafði nær gengið níðið.	The-earl recovered from and found that to-him had near gone the-abuse.	The earl recovered and found that the abuse had come quite close to him.
Sá þá og vegsummerki at af var rotnat skegg allt af jarli og hárið öðrum megin reikar og kom aldrei upp síðan.	Saw then also evidence that off was decayed beard all of the-earl and hair other side parting and came never up since.	He also saw evidence of this, because his beard had decayed, along with the hair on one side of his parting, and it never came back.
Nú lætr jarl ræsta höllina og eru hinu dauðu út bornir.	Now had the-earl cleared the-hall and they-were the dead out carried.	Now the earl had the hall cleared and the dead were carried out.
Þykist hann nú vita at þetta mun Þorleifr verið hafa en karl engi annar og mun launat þykjast hafa honum mannalát og fjártjón.	Thought he now knew that this must Thorleif been had the old-man none other and should repay considered had he manslaughter and financial-loss.	He thought that he knew that the old man must have been none other than Thorleif, and that this was repayment for the manslaughter and his financial loss.
Liggr jarl nú í þessum meinlætum allan þenna vetr og mikið af sumrinu.	Laid the-earl now from this malignance all the winter and most of the-summer.	This malignance laid the earl low for all of the winter and most of the summer.

6

Þat er af Þorleifi at segja at hann snýst til ferðar suðr til Danmerkr og hefir þat til leiðarnests sér sem hann ginnti af þeim í höllinni.	It was of Thorleif to say that he turned to travel south to Denmark and had it to food his as he tricked from them in the-hall.	As for Thorleif, he set to travel south to Denmark, and for his provisions he had the food that he had tricked from them in the hall.

The Tale of Thorlief the Earl's Poet (Old Norse)

Old Norse	Literal	English
En hversu lengi sem hann hefir á leið verið þá létti hann eigi sinni ferð fyrr en hann kom á fund Sveins konungs og tók hann við honum fegins hendi og spurði hann at ferðum sínum en Þorleifr sagði allt sem farið hafði.	Then however long as he had to journey made then relief he not his travel before that he came to find Svein the-king and received he with him relieved hands and asked he of journey his and Thorleif said all which gone had.	Then however long the journey was to be made, he had no relief in his travel until he came to find king Svein, and he received him well with relieved hands, and asked him of his journey, and Thorleif said how all had gone.
Konungr svarar:	The-king answered:	The king answered:
"Nú mun eg lengja nafn þitt og kalla þig Þorleif jarlaskáld".	"Now should i lengthen name yours and call you Thorleif Earl's-Poet".	"Now I should lengthen your name and call you Thorleif the Earl's Poet".
Þá kvat konungr vísu:	Then said the-king verse:	Then the king said a verse:
Grenndi Þorleifr Þrœnda þengils hróðr fyr drengjum, *hafa ólítið ýtar jarls níð borið víða.* *Njörðr réð vestan virðum vellstœri brag fœra brot lands galt gœti grálega leóns báru.*	Slendered Thorleif The-Tronds' the-prince renown before the-fellows, had no-little out the-earl's abuse carried widely. Njord ruled west worthiness well-sized poetry brought away lands repaid got malice the-lion's carried.	Thorleif slendered the Tronds the prince's renown before the fellows, had no-little out the earl's abuse carried widely. Njord ruled the western worth well-sized poetry brought away lands repaid got for the lion's malice carried.
Þorleifr sagði konungi at hann fýstist út til Íslands og beiddi konung orlofs at fara þegar at vori.	Thorleif told the-king that he desired out-from to Iceland and asked the-king vacations to travel there in the-spring.	Thorleif told the king that he wished to travel out to Iceland and asked the king leave to travel there in the spring.
En konungr sagði svo vera skyldu "vil eg gefa þér skip í nafnfesti með mönnum og reiða og þvílíkri áhöfn sem þér þarfast".	Then the-king said so be-it should "wish i to-give you a-ship in name-giving with people and transport and accordingly-like crew as you need".	The king said that it would be so, "I wish to give you a ship as a name-gift, with people and transport and crew as you need".
Nú er Þorleifr þar um veturinn í góðu yfirlœti en at vordögum býr hann skip sitt og lét í haf og byrjaði vel og kom skipi sínu við Ísland í á þá er Þjórsá heitir.	Now was Thorleif there about winter in good favour and of spring-days prepared he ship his and had to sea and began well and came ship his to Iceland in river then was Thjorsa named.	Thorleif was there for the winter in great favour, and at the beginning of spring he prepared his ship and put to sea, and began well and his ship came to Iceland, into the river that was named Thjorsa.

The Tale of Thorlief the Earl's Poet (Old Norse)

Old Norse	Literal	English
Þat segja menn at Þorleifr kvæntist um haustið og fengi þeirrar konu er Auðr hét og væri Þórðar dóttir er bjó í Skógum undir Eyjafjöllum, gilds bónda og stórauðigs, kominn af ætt Þrasa hins gamla.	It is-said people that Thorleif got-married about autumn and got there a-wife who Aud was-named and was Thord daughter that lived in Skogar under Eyjafjoll-Mountains, strong farmer and great-wealth, came of descendents Thrasi the old.	People say that Thorleif got married in the autumn and had a wife who was named Aud, and she was the daughter of Thord of Skogar under the Eyjafjoll mountains, who was a successful and wealthy farmer, descended from Thrasi the old.
Auðr var kvenskörungr mikill.	Aud was noble-woman much.	Aud was very much a noble woman.
Þorleifr sat um veturinn í Skógum en um vorið eftir keypti hann land at Höfðabrekku í Mýdal og bjó þar síðan.	Thorleif sat about winter in Skogar but about spring afterwards bought he land at Hofdabrekka in Myrdal-Valley and settled there since.	Thorleif spent the winter in Skogar, but the following spring he bought land at Hofdabrekka in the Myrdal valley and settled thereafter.

7

En nú er þar til at taka er Hákon jarl er, at honum batnaði hins mesta meinlœtis en þat segja sumir menn at hann yrði aldrei samr maðr og áðr og vildi jarl nú gjarna hefna Þorleifi þessar smánar ef hann gœti, heitir nú á fulltrúa sína, Þorgerði Hörgabrúði og Irpu systr hennar, at reka þann galdr út til Íslands at Þorleifi ynni at fullu og fœrir þeim miklar fórnir og gekk til frétta.	But now is there to from take that Hakon the-earl was, that he bettered his most malignancy but that said some people that he became never the-same man of before and wished the-earl now gladly avenge Thorleif this humiliation if he could, called now on delegates his, Thorgerd Horgabrudi and Irpu sister hers, to drive then sorcery out to Iceland to Thorleif win-over that full and carried them much sacrifices and got to omens.	Now to take to the Earl Hakon, he mostly recovered from this malignancy, but some people said that he was never the same man as before, and the earl now wished to gladly avenge Thorleif of this humiliation if he could, he called on his delegates, Thorgerd Horgabrudi and her sister Irpu, to drive sorcery out to Iceland to defeat Thorleif fully, and he carried them many offerings and got omens.

The Tale of Thorlief the Earl's Poet (Old Norse)

Old Norse	Literal	English
En er hann fékk þá frétt er honum líkaði lét hann taka einn rekabút og gera úr trémann og með fjölkynngi og atkvæðum jarls en tröllskap og fítonsanda þeirra systra lét hann drepa einn mann og taka úr hjartat og láta í þenna trémann og fœrðu síðan í föt og gáfu nafn og kölluðu Þorgarð og mögnuðu hann með svo miklum fjandans krafti at hann gekk og mælti við menn, komu honum síðan í skip og sendu hann út til Íslands þess erindis at drepa Þorleif jarlaskáld.	And when he got then omens that he liked had he taken a drift-wood and made of wooden-man and with witchcraft and songs earls and witchcraft and magic there sisters had he kill one man and taken out heart and had in this wooden-man and brought afterwards to clothing and gave name and called Thorgard and power he with so much devil's power that he walked and talked with people, came to-him afterwards to a-ship and sent him out to Iceland this errand to kill Thorleif Earl's-Poet.	And when he got the omens that he liked, he took some drift wood and made a wooden man, and with his witchcraft and songs, and with the magic of his sisters, he had a man killed to take his heart and place in the wooden man, and afterwards brought clothing and gave him a name and called him Thorgard, and with the strong power of the devil he walked and talked with people, he was put on a ship and sent to Iceland on an errand to kill Thorleif the Earl's poet.
Gyrti Hákon hann atgeir þeim er hann hafði tekið úr hofi þeirra systra og Hörgi hafði átt.	Equipped Hakon him a-halberd then that he had taken out-of temple theirs sisters and Horgi had belonged.	Hakon gave him a halberd that he had taken out of the temple that belonged to his sisters at Horgi.
Þorgarðr kom út til Íslands í þann tíma er menn voru á alþingi.	Thorgard came out to Iceland in that time that men were in assembly.	Thorgard came to Iceland at the time when people were at the assembly.
Þorleifr jarlaskáld var á þingi.	Thorleif Earl's-Poet was at assembly.	Thorleif's the Earl's Poet was at the assembly.
Þat var einn dag at Þorleifr gekk frá búð sinni er hann sá at maðr gekk vestan yfir Öxará.	It was one day that Thorleif went from booth his when he saw that a-man walked from-the-west over Oxara.	One day Thorleif went from his booth and saw a man walking from the west over the Oxara river.
Sá var mikill vexti og illslegr í bragði.	Saw was large grown and evil-like in movement.	He saw that he was large and evil looking in his movement.
Þorleifr spyr þenna mann at heiti.	Thorleif asked this man of name.	Thorleif asked this man his name.
Hann nefndist Þorgarðr og kastaði þegar kaldyrðum at Þorleifi en er Þorleifr heyrði þat ætlaði hann at bregða sverðinu konungsnaut er hann var gyrðr með en í þessu bili lagði Þorgarðr atgeirnum á Þorleifi miðjum og í gegnum hann.	He was-named Thorgard and cast straightaway cold-bloodedly to Thorleif and when Thorleif heard this intended he to draw the-sword king's-gift that he was equipped-with with but in this moment laid Thorgard halberd to Thorleif's middle and in through him.	He said that his name was Thorgard and looked at him cold-bloodedly, and when Thorleif heard this, he intended to draw the sword that king Svein had given to him, but in that moment, Thorgard laid his halberd through his middle.

The Tale of Thorlief the Earl's Poet (Old Norse)

Old Norse	Literal	English
En er hann fékk lagið hjó hann til Þorgarðs en hann steyptist í jörðina niðr svo at í iljarnar var at sjá.	Then when he got laid struck he to Thorgard then he disappeared into the-earth down so that for soles-of-the-feet was to see.	Then when he was hit, he struck at Thorgard, but he had disappeared down into the earth so that only the soles of his feet could be seen.
Þorleifr snaraði at sér kyrtilinn og kvat vísu:	Thorleif twisted about himself tunic and spoke verse:	Thorleif twisted his tunic about him and spoke a verse:
Hvarf hinn hildardjarfi, hvat varð af Þorgarði? villumaðr á velli, vígdjarfr refilstiga.	Disappeared the courageous-warrior, what became of Thorgard villain in the-fields, slaying-warrior mysterious-path.	The courageous warrior disappeared, what became of Thorgard? the villain in the fields, the slaying warrior's mysterious path.
Farið hefir Gautr at grjóti gunnelds hinn fjölkunni, síðan mun hann í helju hvílast stund og mílu.	Gone has Odin to rocks battle-fire the skilled-in-magic, after shall he in Hel rest awhile and mile.	Odin has gone to the rocks, battle-fired the skills in magic, after shall be in Hel and rest awhile a mile.
Þá gekk Þorleifr heim til búðar sinnar og sagði mönnum þenna atburð og þótti öllum mikils um vert um þenna atburð.	Then went Thorleif home to booth his and told people these events and thought all much about had-been about these events.	Thorleif went back to his booth and told people of these events, and people thought much about these events.
Síðan varpar Þorleifr frá sér kyrtlinum og féllu þá út iðrin og lét Þorleifr þar líf sitt við góðan orðstír og þótti mönnum þat allmikill skaði.	Afterwards threw Thorleif from himself tunic and fell then out bowels and laid Thorleif there life his with good fame and thought people that all-great harm.	Afterwards Thorleif threw off his tunic and his bowels spilled out, and he laid his life there with good fame, and all people thought that this was a great harm.
Þóttust nú allir vita at Þorgarðr þessi hafði engi verið annar en galdr og fjölkynngi Hákonar jarls.	Thought now all certainly that Thorgard this had none been other than sorcery and witchcraft Hakon's the-earl.	They thought that it was certain that this Thorgard had been none other than the sorcery and witchcraft of Earl Hakon.
Síðan var Þorleifr heygðr.	Afterwards was Thorleif buried.	Afterwards Thorleif was buried.
Haugr hans stendr norðr af lögréttu og sést hann enn.	Mound his stood north of law-assembly and seen he was.	His mound stood north of the law assembly and could be seen from there.

The Tale of Thorlief the Earl's Poet (Old Norse)

Old Norse	Literal	English
Brœðr hans voru á þingi er þetta var tíðinda og gerðu útferð Þorleifs sœmilega og erfðu hann at fornum sið en Ásgeir faðir þeirra var þá litlu andaðr.	Brothers his was at assembly when this was news and made funeral Thorleif's fair and inherited he the ancient traditions as Asgeir father theirs was then recently died.	His brothers were at the assembly when this became news, and they gave Thorleif a fair funeral feast according to the ancient traditions that his father Asgeir had when he recently died.
Síðan fóru menn heim af þingi og fréttust þessi tíðindi nú víða um Ísland og þóttu mikils verð.	Afterwards went people home from assembly and reported this news now widely about Iceland and thought a-great price.	Afterwards people went home from the assembly and reported this news widely about Iceland, and everyone thought it a great cost.

8

Old Norse	Literal	English
Sá maðr bjó þá á Þingvelli er Þorkell hét.	So a-man lived then at Thingvellir who-was Thorkell named.	So there was a man who lived that Thingvellir and was named Thorkell.
Hann var auðigr maðr at ganganda fé og hafði jafnan hœgt í búi.	He was wealthy man as went cattle and had equally comfortable in farm.	He was a wealth man with regard to cattle, and had a comfortable farm.
Engi var hann virðingamaðr.	None was he man-of-high-rank.	He was not a man of high rank.
Sauðamaðr hans hét Hallbjörn og var kallaðr hali.	Shepherd his named Hallbjorn and was called Hali.	He shepherd was named Hallbjorn but people called him Hali (Tail).
Hann vandist oftlega til at koma á haug Þorleifs og svaf þar um nœtr og hélt þar nálœgt fé sínu.	He did often to that came to mound Thorleif's and slept there about night and held there close cattle his.	He often came to Thorleif's mound and slept there through the night and held his cattle close there.
Kemr honum þat jafnan í hug at hann vildi geta ort lof kvœði nokkurt um haugbúann og talar þat jafnan er hann liggr á hauginum en sakir þess at hann var ekki skáld og hann hafði þeirrar listar eigi fengið fékk hann ekki kveðið og komst aldrei lengra áfram fyrir honum um skáldskapinn en hann byrjaði svo:	Came he that equally in thoughts that he wished get words praise poem some about the-mound-dweller and said that usually when he lay about the-mound but for-the-sake this that he was not poet and he had there art not got went he not poem but came never longer not-further for him about poetry that he began so:	Thoughts often came to him that he wished to compose words of praise about the mound dweller, and he usually said so when he lay about the mound, but because he was not a good poet and did not have the gift, he never managed to compose anything longer than the beginning:
Hér liggr skáld.	Here lies a-poet.	Here lies a poet.

The Tale of Thorlief the Earl's Poet (Old Norse)

Old Norse	Literal	English
En meira gat hann ekki kveðið.	Then more could he not put-to-words.	Then he could not put more to words.
Þat var eina nátt sem oftar at hann liggr á hauginum og hefir hina sömu iðn fyrir stafni ef hann gœti aukið nokkuð lof um haugbúann.	It was one night as often that he laid about the-mound and had then same craft for staves if he got increase some praise about the-mound-dweller.	One night as usual he was lying on the mound and was still trying to craft some verses and write any more in praise about the mound dweller.
Síðan sofnar hann og eftir þat sér hann at opnast haugurinn og gengr þar út maðr mikill vexti og vel búinn.	Afterwards slept he and after that saw he that open the-mound and went there out a-man great grown and well prepared.	Then he fell asleep and after that he saw that the mound opened, and a large man came out, and he was well dressed.
Hann gekk upp á hauginn at Hallbirni og mælti:	He went up to the-mound to Hallbjorn and spoke:	He went up to the mound and said to Hallbjorn:
"Þar liggr Hallbjörn og vildir þú fást í því sem þér er ekki lánat, at yrkja lof um mig og er þat annaðhvort at þér verðr lagið í þessi íþrótt og munt þú þat af mér fá meira en vel flestum mönnum öðrum og er þat vænna at svo verði ella þarftu ekki í þessu at brjótast lengr.	"There lies Hallbjorn and wish you get with therefore which you are not gifted, that compose praise about me and is that either-way that you become have of this skilled and shall you that of me have more than well most people others and is that good that so becomes or need not of this to break longer.	"There you lie, Hallbjorn, and you would like to catch something not in your power, to compose praise about me, and either you will become skilled and you can get this from me more than others, as is likely to happen, or else there is no need for you to continue any longer.
Skal eg nú kveða fyrir þér vísu og ef þú getr numið vísuna og kannt hana þá er þú vaknar þá munt þú verða þjóðskáld og yrkja lof um marga höfðingja og mun þér í þessi íþrótt mikið lagið verða".	Shall i now speak before you verse and if you can take verse and know it then when you awake then shall you become skilled-poet and compose praise about many chieftains and should you in this skilled much have become".	I shall now speak a verse for you, and if you can take this verse and know it, then when you awake, you shall become a skilled poet and compose praise about many chieftains, and you shall have become much skilled in this".
Síðan togar hann á honum tunguna og kvat vísu þessa:	Afterwards pulled he of his tongue and spoke verse this:	Then he pulled his tongue and spoke this verse:
Hér liggr skáld þat er skálda	Here lies poet that is of-poets	Here lies a poet that is of all poets
skörungr var mestr at flestu.	leading was the-greatest of the-most.	the leading, he was the greatest of the most.
Naddveiti frá eg nýtan	Provided-knowing from i am-able	I hear that he was able
níð Hákoni smíða.	abuse of-Hakon created.	to craft abuse of Hakon.

The Tale of Thorlief the Earl's Poet (Old Norse)

Old Norse	Literal	English
Áðr gat engr né síðan annarra svo manna, frægt hefir orðið þat fyrðum, férán lokið hánum.	After got none nor afterwards others so people, fame had words that warriors, plunder end his.	None before or after, of so many other people, had fame of words that warriors ended his plunder.
"Nú skaltu svo hefja skáldskapinn at þú skalt yrkja lofkvœði um mig þá er þú vaknar og vanda sem mest bœði hátt og orðfœri og einna mest kenningar".	"Now shall so begin poetry that you shall compose praise-words about me then when you awake and care that most both high and vocabulary and only the-best kennings".	"Now you shall begin your poetry that you shall compose words of praise about me, then when you awake, take care that it is both high in vocabulary and the best kennings".
Síðan hverfr hann aftr í hauginn og lýkst hann aftr en Hallbjörn vaknar og þykist sjá á herðar honum.	Afterwards turned he back into the-mound and closed he returned then Hallbjorn awoke and thought saw of shoulders his.	Afterwards he turned back into the mound and it closed behind him, then Hallbjorn awoke and thought he saw his shoulders.
Síðan kunni hann vísuna og fór síðan til byggða heim með fé sitt eftir tíma og sagði þenna atburð.	Afterwards knew he verse and travelled since to settlement home with wealth his after time and said then events.	Afterwards he remembered the verse and then went back to the farm with his flock after a time and told of these events.
Orti Hallbjörn síðan lofkvœði um haugbúann og var hið mesta skáld og fór utan fljótlega og kvat kvœði um marga höfðingja og fékk af þeim miklar virðingar og góðar gjafir og grœddi af því stórfé, og gengr af honum mikil saga bœði hér á landi og útlendis þó at hún sé hér eigi rituð.	Words Hallbjorn since praise-words about the-mound-dweller and was then the-best poet and travelled out soon and spoke poems about many chieftains and got of them much honour and good gifts and profit of therefore great-wealth, and went of him much stories both here about the-land and other-lands though that it being here not written.	Hallbjorn composed since words of praise about the mound dweller and was the best poet, and he frequently travelled abroad and composed poems about many chieftains and received from them much honour and good gifts from them, and his wealth increased, and there went many stories about him both in Iceland and abroad, but they are not written down here.
En frá brœðrum Þorleifs er þat at segja at nœsta sumar eftir andlát hans fóru þeir utan, Ólafr völubrjótr og Helgi hinn frœkni, og œtluðu til hefnda eftir bróðr sinn.	Then from brothers Thorlief's was it to say that next summer after death his travelled they out, Olaf knuckle-breaker and Helgi the brave, and supposed to revenge after brother theirs.	Then to Thorlief's brothers to say that the next summer after his death day, Olaf knuckle-breaker and Helgi the brave travelled out and intended to get revenge for their brother.
En þeim varð eigi lagið þá enn at standa yfir höfuðsvörðum Hákonar jarls því at hann hafði þá enn eigi öllu illu því fram farið sem honum varð lagið sér til skammar og skaða.	But they were not laid then but to stand over head-skin Hakon's the-earl because that he had then but not all evil such from going as he was laid to-him to shame and damage.	But they were not yet fated to have Earl Hakon's scalp, because he had not yet done all of the evil which was destined for his shame and harm.

The Tale of Thorlief the Earl's Poet (Old Norse)

Old Norse	Literal	English
En þó brenndu þeir mörg hof fyrir jarlinum og gerðu honum margan fjárskaða í ránum og hervirki er þeir veittu honum og margri annarri óspekt.	But though burned they many temples for the-earl and did to-him many wealth-damage in robbery and plundering that they granted him and many other disturbances.	But they managed to burn many of the earl's temples, and did much to damage his wealth with robbery and plundering, and they granted him many other disturbances.
Og lýkr hér frá Þorleifi at segja.	And ends here from Thorleif to say.	And this is the end of what there is to say about Thorlief.

Word List *(Old Norse to English)*

Old Norse	English
A, a	
aðfangskveld	midwinter-evening
aðrar	other
aðrir	other, others
af	from, in, of, off
afliðið	following
aftr	after, back, returned, returning
afturreka	back-driven
aldr	age
aldrei	never
aldri	age
alfari	for-good
alla	all
allan	all
allir	all
allmikill	all-great
allri	all
alls	all
allt	all
alþingi	assembly
andaðr	died
andar	soul
andlát	death
andvana	destitution
annaðhvort	either-way
annan	a-second
annar	another, other
annarra	other, others
annarri	other
annars	another's
at	a, about, and, as, at, for, from, in, it, of, that, the, then, this, to
atburð	events
atburðir	events
atgeir	a-halberd
atgeirnum	halberd
atgervi	deeds
atgervimaðr	accomplished-man
atkvæðum	songs
auðigr	wealthy
Auðr	Aud (name)
aukið	increase
austr	east
Á, á	
á	about, at, for, from, had, in, it, of, on, river, that, this, to
áðr	after, before, return
áfram	not-further
áhöfn	crew
án	without
ánauð	enslavement
Ásgeir	Asgeir (name)
Ásgeiri	Asgeir (name)
ásjá	assistance
ástfóstr	foster-care
ásum	poles
át	eat
átján	eighteen
átt	belonged, had
áttu	had
B, b	
báðir	both
bani	dead
báru	carried
bat	asked, bid, invited
batna	better
batnaði	bettered
báts	boats
beiddi	asked
beiddist	asked
bekkjunauta	bench-fellows
betr	better
biðr	asked
bili	moment
binda	bound, tied-up

Word List (Old Norse to English)

Old Norse	English
bindr	bound
bjart	bright
bjó	lived, prepared, settled
blekkir	deceived
Blönduósi	Blonduos (place)
blygðar	shame
boðið	invited
bœði	both
bœginn	troubled
böggva	the-mauler
bölvaðra	cursed
bónda	farmer
borð	the-tables
borið	carried
bornir	carried
bráðlega	quickly
brag	poetry
bragði	movement
branda	swords
bregða	draw
bregðr	tricked
Brekku	Brekka (place)
brenna	burned, burnt
brenndu	burned
brjótast	break
broddr	spikes
bróðr	brother
brœðr	brothers
brœðrum	brothers
brot	away
brott	away
búð	booth
búðanna	booths
búðar	booth
búi	farm
búið	done, settled
búinn	prepared
búkinn	body
burt	away
byggða	settlement
býr	prepared
byrjaði	began
byrjar	fair-wind
býsn	strangeness

D, d

Old Norse	English
dag	day
daginn	the-day
dálegra	harmful
Danmerkr	Denmark (place)
dauðu	dead
diska	plates
dœmt	deem
dögum	days
dökkri	dark
dóttir	daughter
draga	drew
drápu	phrases
dregr	drawn, draws
drekktr	drowned
drengjum	the-fellows
drengr	men
drepa	kill
drykkju	drink
drykkjuborð	drinking-tables
dýflissu	dungeon
dýrstum	dearest
dyrum	doors

E, e

Old Norse	English
eða	either, or
eðli	nature
ef	if
efnilegir	promising
efsta	upper
eftir	after, afterwards
eftirmáls	after-the-case
eg	i, if
eiga	not
eigi	not
eigið	own
eign	owning
eina	a, one
einn	a, one
einna	only
Eiríks	Erik s (name)
ekki	not

Word List (Old Norse to English)

Old Norse	English
ella	or
elli	age
ellina	age
elsti	eldest
en	and, as, but, than, that, the, then, when
enda	and, end
engi	none
Englandi	England (place)
engr	none
enn	but, was
er	am, are, as, from, has, is, it-is, that, the, was, what, when, which, who, who-was
erfðu	inherited
erindis	errand
ertu	are-you
eru	are, they-were, we-are
eta	eat
etið	to-eat
Eyjafjöllum	Eyjafjoll-Mountains (place)
eymd	misery
eyri	sand

É, é

él	blizzard

F, f

Old Norse	English
fá	get, have
faðir	father
Fagurkinn	Fair-Cheek (name)
fann	found
fara	travel
fararefna	travel-goods
farið	going, gone, travelled
farning	passage
fast	close, closed, closely
fást	get
fé	cattle, wealth
fegins	relieved
fékk	got, went
félaga	companions
féll	fell
fellr	fell
féllu	fell
fengi	got
fengið	caught, got
fer	travelled, went
férán	plunder
ferð	travel
ferðar	travel
ferðum	journey
fertuga	forty
festist	grips
fíl	elephant
finnr	found
fítonsanda	magic
fjandans	devil's
fjárhlut	fee-lot, financial-share
fjárskaða	wealth-damage
fjártjón	financial-loss
fjölkunni	skilled-in-magic
fjölkynngi	witchcraft
fjölmenni	following-men
fleira	more
flestu	the-most
flestum	most
fljótasta	soonest
fljótlega	soon
flutt	performed
flytja	to-carry
flyttu	move
föðr	father
fœ	can, get
fœra	bring, brought
fœrðu	brought
fœrir	carried
fór	travelled, went
fornfrœði	ancient-ways
fórnir	sacrifices
fornlegum	ancient-ways
fornum	ancient
forsmáðr	shamed
fóru	travelled, went
förunauta	companions

Word List (Old Norse to English)

Old Norse	English
fóstra	foster-father
fóstri	fostered
föt	clothing
frá	from
fram	forward, from
framan	in-front-of
framaverka	previous-deeds
framleiðslu	causing
frásagnar	from-told
frétt	omens
fréttar	omens
fréttist	sought
fréttust	reported
frœðum	instruction
frœgt	fame
frœkni	brave
frœnda	kinsmen
fullkomið	full-coming
fulltingi	assistance
fulltrúa	delegates
fullu	full
fund	find, meet
fylgdi	followed
fylgt	followed
fyr	before
fyrðum	warriors
fyrir	before, before him, for
fyrr	before
fyrst	first
fýsi	desire
fýstist	desired

G, g

Old Norse	English
gáði	cared
gaf	gave
gáfu	gave
gáir	care
galdr	sorcery
galt	repaid
gamall	old
gamla	old
gamlir	old-man
ganga	go, went
ganganda	went
gangi	moved
Gáseyri	Gaseyri (place)
gat	could, got
Gautr	Odin (name)
geðjast	liking
gefa	give, to-give
gegnum	through
geitarskegg	goat-beard
geitarskegginu	goat-beard
gekk	got, walked, went
gengið	gone
gengr	going, went
ger	made
gera	done, made
gerði	did, had-done, it-was
gerðist	happened
gerðu	did, made
gerist	becoming
gerningum	witchcraft
gert	done
gervi	character
gervilegr	talented
gervina	disguise
geta	get
getið	told-of
getr	can, get
geysimjǫk	exceedingly-much
giftu	luck
gildr	capable
gilds	strong
gíman	opening
ginnti	tricked
gjafir	gifts
gjalda	repay
gjallandason	son-of-gjallandi
gjarna	gladly
gjöld	repayment
glögglega	clearly
goða	the-chieftain
góða	food
góðan	good
góðar	good
goði	chieftain
góðu	good, improvement
gœti	could, got

Word List (Old Norse to English)

Old Norse	English
göldrum	magical-arts
gömlum	old
góss	belongings
gott	good
grálega	malice
gramr	warrior
greiðlega	promptly, quickly
grenndi	slendered
grjóti	rocks
grœddi	profit
guðníðingskapr	idol-worship
Guðs	God (name)
gulls	of-gold
gunnelds	battle-fire
gyrðr	equipped-with
gyrti	equipped

H, h

Old Norse	English
haf	sea
hafa	had, have
hafði	had
hafi	have
hafið	have
haft	have
Hákon	Hakon (name)
Hákonar	Hakon (name), Hakon's (name)
hákoni	of-Hakon
halda	hold
hálf	half
Hali	Hali (name)
Hallbirni	Hallbjorn (name)
Hallbjörn	Hallbjorn (name)
hálminn	the-straw
hana	it
hann	he, him
hans	he, his
hánum	his
harðfengi	toughness
harðla	hardly
harðleikinn	rough
harðúðigr	harsher
háreysti	commotion
hárið	hair
hark	noise
háseta	first-mate
hásetum	crew
hataðr	hated
hátt	high
háttum	custom
haug	mound
haugbúann	the-mound-dweller
hauginn	the-mound
hauginum	the-mound
haugr	mound
haugurinn	the-mound
haustið	autumn
hefi	have
hefir	had, has, have, having
hefja	begin
hefna	avenge
hefnda	revenge
hefr	had
hegningartíminn	punishment-time
heim	home, homes
heita	call, named, promise
heiti	name, named
heitir	called, named
heldr	rather
Helgi	Helgi (name)
heljarkarl	hellish-old-man
Helju	Hel (place)
hélt	held
hendi	hands
hengja	hanged
hennar	hers, its
hentar	requirements
hentugri	more-convenient
hér	here
herðar	shoulders
herra	lord
hervirki	plundering
hét	named, promised, was-named
heygðr	buried
heyrði	heard
heyrðu	heard
heyrið	hear
heyrt	heard

Word List (Old Norse to English)

Old Norse	English
hið	the, then
hildardjarfi	courageous-warrior
himins	heaven's
hina	then
hingat	here
hinn	the, those
hinni	the
hins	his, the
hinu	the
hinum	other
hít	bag
hítina	the-bag
hitti	met
hjartat	heart
hjó	struck
Hlaðajarl	Earl-Of-Lade (name)
Hlaðajarls	Earl-Of-Lade (name)
Hlaðir	Lade (place)
hleypr	ran
Hlöðum	Lade (place)
hlógu	laughed
hlýða	listen, to-hear
hlýdduð	listen-to
hœgt	comfortable, possible
hœkjr	crutches
hœkjurnar	the-crutches
hof	temples
hóf	began
Höfðabrekku	Hofdabrekka (place)
höfðingja	chieftains, chieftains'
höfðingjum	chieftains
höfðingskap	lordship
hofi	temple
höfuðsvörðum	head-skin
höfum	have
höllina	the-hall
höllinni	the-hall
honum	he, he-had, him, his, to-him
Hörgabrúði	Horgabrudi (name)
Hörgi	Horgi (place)
hríð	awhile
hrífa	scratched
hring	a-ring
hróðr	renown
hrollir	shivering

Old Norse	English
hrukku	drew
hug	thoughts
hugr	heart
hugsa	think
hún	it, she
hvarf	disappeared
hvat	what
hver	who
hverfr	turned
hvergi	each
hverjum	each, who's
hvern	one's
hverri	each
hversu	however, how-so
hvert	each
hví	why
hvílast	rest
hvorri	each
hvort	whether

I, i

Old Norse	English
iðn	craft
iðrin	bowels
iljarnar	soles-of-the-feet
illa	bad, badly, ill
illr	bad, ill
illslegr	evil-like
illu	evil
inn	in
Irpu	Irpu (name)

Í, í

Old Norse	English
í	about, at, for, from, in, into, of, to, with
Ísland	Iceland (place)
Íslandi	Iceland (place)
Íslands	Iceland (place)
íþrótt	skilled
íþrótta	skills
íþróttamaðr	excellent-man
íþróttir	skilled
ítri	high-born

Word List (Old Norse to English)

Old Norse	English

J, j

jafnan	equally, usually
jarl	earl, the-earl
Jarlaskáld	Earl's-Poet (name)
jarli	earl, the-earl
jarlinn	the-earl
jarlinum	the-earl
jarls	earls, the-earl, the-earl's
jarlsníði	the-earl's-abuse
jarlsníðs	earl's-abuse
járn	iron-weapon
Jóla	Yule (name)
jólaveislunnar	yule-feast
jörðina	the-earth
Jóta	Jutland (place)

K, k

kaldyrðum	cold-bloodedly
kalla	call, called, call-to
kallaðr	called
kann	can
kannt	know
Karl	Karl (name), old-man, the-old-man
karli	man, the-old-man
kastaði	cast
kaupir	bought
kaupmönnum	trading-men
kaupslagar	bargaining
kaupstaðinn	market-town
kaupunauta	customers
kaupunautar	customers
kemr	came, comes
kenna	teach
kenndr	known
kenningar	kennings
keypti	bought
kláði	itching
Klaufa	Klaufi (name)
knarrar	merchant-ships, of-the-ship
knúta	knots
kol	the-coals
köld	cold
köldu	cold
köldum	cold
kölluðu	called
kolum	coals
kom	came, come, could
koma	came, come, come-with
komast	come
kömbum	combs
komi	comes
kominn	came, comes, coming
komst	came
komu	came
kona	a-woman, wife, woman
Konrvísr	Woman-Verses (name)
konu	a-wife
konung	the-king
konungi	the-king
konungr	the-king
konungs	the-king
konungsnaut	king's-gift
kost	food, provide
krafti	power
krókóttum	devious
kunni	knew
kvaddi	greeted
kvaðningar	greeting
kvala	torment
kvat	said, spoke
kveða	recites, say, speak
kveðið	poem, put-to-words, spoken
kveðr	said
kveldið	evening
kvenskörungr	noble-woman
kvœði	poem, poems
kvœðið	poem, the-poem
kvœðislaunum	poem's-reward
kvœntist	got-married

Word List (Old Norse to English)

Old Norse	English
kyndugskap	cunning
kynferði	kinsmen-origins
kynjaðr	descended
kynstrum	strange
kyrr	sit-still
kyrtilinn	tunic
kyrtlinum	tunic

L, l

Old Norse	English
lagasetning	legislation
lagði	had, laid
lagið	have, laid
lánat	gifted
land	land, the-land
landi	the-land
lands	lands
lásum	locks
lát	let
láta	allow, had
láti	had
látið	let
laun	secrecy
launat	repay
legið	laying
leið	journey, passed
leiðarnests	food
leitaði	sought
lengi	long
lengja	lengthen
lengr	for-long, longer
lengra	longer
leóns	the-lion's
lét	had, laid, let
létti	relief
leysa	solve
líf	life
lífsdaga	life-days
lífstíma	lifetime
liggr	laid, lay, lies
líkaði	liked
líkama	body
líkar	like
linnir	stopped
listar	art

Old Norse	English
lítillœti	a-little, humility
lítils	little
lítinn	little
litlu	recently
Ljótólfi	Ljotolf (name)
Ljótólfr	Ljotolf (name)
Ljótólfs	Ljotolf (name)
ljótu	ghastly
lœtr	had, left
lof	praise
lofaði	praised
lofkvœði	praise-words
lögréttu	law-assembly
lokið	end
luktum	shut
lýkr	ends
lýkst	closed

M, m

Old Norse	English
má	may
maðr	a-man, man
mál	matter
mann	man
manna	man's, men, people
mannalát	manslaughter
manni	people
mannillska	man-evil
manninn	people
marga	many
margan	many
margir	many
margkunnandi	many-known
margra	many, much
margri	many
mart	many
matar	food
mátti	may
með	with
mega	may
megi	may
megin	side
meinlœtis	malignancy
meinlœtum	malignance
meir	more

Word List (Old Norse to English)

Old Norse	English
meira	more
menn	men, people
mér	i-am, me, to-me
mest	most, the-best
mesta	most, the-best
mesti	most
mestr	the-greatest
miðdigr	broad-waist
Miðfirði	Midfjord (place)
Miðfjarðar-Skeggja	Midfjorder-Skeggi (name)
miðju	middle-of
miðjum	middle
miðs	middle
mig	me, shall-i
mikið	most, much
mikil	much
mikill	great, large, much
mikils	a-great, much
mikinn	much
mikla	much
miklar	much
miklum	much
milli	between
mílu	mile
minn	mine
minnkaði	decreased
mislíkaði	misliked
missa	miss
mitt	mine
mjǫk	much
móðr	mother
móðrbróðr	mother's-brother
mælt	said
mælti	spoke, talked
mögnuðu	power
mökkr	thick-clouds
mönnum	men, people, peoples'
mörg	many
mörgum	many
morguninn	morning
mörk	a-mark
mörkum	marshes
mun	must, shall, should
mundi	would
mundu	would
munn	mouth
munt	shall
munuð	shall, should
munum	shall
Mýdal	Myrdal-Valley (place)
myrkrið	the-darkness
myrkt	dark

N, n

Old Norse	English
naddveiti	provided-knowing
náði	caught
naðrbings	dragon
nafn	name
nafnfesti	name-giving
nafni	name
nákvæmi	pernickety
nálægt	close
nam	took
náms	take
nátt	night
náttúra	nature
né	nor
nefndist	was-named
nema	except, taken, unless
níð	abuse
níðið	the-abuse
niðr	down
Níðungr	Nidung (name)
nítján	nineteen
Njörðr	Njord (name)
nœr	near
nœsta	next
nœstir	nearest
nœtr	night
nokkr	anything
nokkuð	any, some, something, somewhat
nokkura	some
nokkurar	some
nokkurt	some
nökkvi	the-ship
norðr	north
Noreg	Norway (place)
Noregs	Norway (place)

Word List (Old Norse to English)

Old Norse	English
nóttina	the-night
nú	now
numið	take
nýtan	am-able

O, o

Old Norse	English
ofan	over
ofanverðum	the-uppermost
ofléttlega	willingly
oft	often
oftar	often
oftlega	often
og	also, and, but, of
opnast	open
orð	words
orðfœri	vocabulary
orðið	become, words
orðskvið	proverb
orðstír	fame
orlof	leave
orlofs	vacations
ort	worded, words
orti	words
oss	us, we

Ó, ó

Old Norse	English
óbœtilegs	un-redeemable
óðali	estate
ófreklegar	un-eagerly
ógert	undone
ógladdist	un-gladdened
ógleði	un-gladness
ógleðr	un-glad
óhljóði	unsoundly
óhöfðinglegt	chieftain-like
ókunna	unknown
Ólafr	Olaf (name)
Ólafs	Olaf's (name)
ólítið	no-little
óloknum	undone
óminnis	amnesia
óspekt	disturbances

Old Norse	English
óvant	not-lacking
óvinarins	the-enemy's
óvit	unconsciousness
óvœra	restlessness
óvœri	restlessness

Ö, ö

Old Norse	English
öðlings	noble
öðrum	other, others
öldu	wave
öllu	all
öllum	all, of-all
önga	none
öngu	not
örleik	generosity
örverpi	decrepitude
örvœnt	desperation
Öxará	Oxara (place)

Œ, œ

Old Norse	English
œfr	angry
œrnri	merry
œti	ate, had
œtlaði	intenced
œtluðu	supposed
œtt	ancestors, ancestry, descendents
œvintýr	adverture

P, p

Old Norse	English
peninga	money

R, r

Old Norse	English
ráðum	advice
raknaði	recovered
ránum	robbery
Rauðfeldr	Red-Cloak (name)
Rauði	Red (name)

Word List (Old Norse to English)

Old Norse	English
réð	ruled
refilstiga	mysterious-path
reiða	transport
reikar	parting
reka	drive
rekabút	drift-wood
Reykjum	Reykir (place)
reyndar	actually
ríða	rose
ríkr	powerful
rís	rose
rituð	written
roðið	reddened
röðla	wheel
rœðr	hired
rœndi	robbed
rœsta	cleared
rotnat	decayed
ryðja	cleared
ryðr	cleared

S, s

Old Norse	English
sá	saw, so
saga	stories
sagði	said, told
sagðr	said
sagt	said
sakir	for-the-sake, sake, with-conviction
saman	together
samr	the-same
samsœtis	banquet
sannlega	truly
sat	sat
satt	true
sauðamaðr	shepherd
sé	being, himself, see
segðu	say-you
segið	said
segir	said
segist	say
segja	is-said, said, say
seigt	tough
selja	to-sell
sem	as, that, what, which
sendu	sent
sér	for-himself, he, he-himself, him, himself, his, saw, to-him
sest	sat
sést	seen
sið	traditions
síðan	after, afterwards, since
síðasta	last
síðr	less
sig	him
sigldu	sailed
sína	himself, his
sinn	his, theirs
sinna	his
sinnar	his
sinni	himself, his
síns	his
sínu	his
sínum	his
sitt	his
sjá	saw, see
sjálfráða	ourselves-decide
skaða	damage
skaði	harm
skal	shall
skáld	a-poet, poet
skálda	of-poets
skaldi	the-poet
skáldskap	poetry
skáldskapinn	poetry
skalt	shall
skaltu	shall, shall-you
skammar	shame
skapaðir	shaped
skegg	beard
Skeggi	Skeggi (name)
Skeggja	Skeggi (name)
skildu	parted
skip	a-ship, ship
skipaði	arranged
skipi	ship
skipið	the-ship
skips	ship, ships

Word List (Old Norse to English)

Old Norse	English
skipti	exchanged
skjóta	launched
skógum	forests, Skogar (place)
skörulega	boldly
skörungr	leading, noble
skruma	show-off, swagger
skyldi	should
skyldr	should
skyldu	should
sléttri	levelled
slíkt	such
slægða	slyness
smánar	humiliation
smíða	created
snaraði	twisted
snemma	early-age
snýr	turned
snýst	turned
sækja	sake
sællífi	blessed-life
sæmd	honour
sæmilega	fair, properly
sæti	sit
sætis	sit
sofnar	slept
sögðu	said
sögr	sagas
sögu	saga
sölr	sale
sömu	same
son	son
sonar	son
sótt	sought
spurði	asked, learned
spurn	learned
spurt	learned
spyr	asked, asks, learned
spyrja	ask
staðið	stand
stafina	sticks
stafkarl	beggar
stafkarla	beggars
stafkarlar	beggars
stafkarls	as-a-beggar, beggar's
stafni	staves

Old Norse	English
standa	stand, stood
stef	stave
stendr	stood
steyptist	disappeared
stóð	stood
stóra	large
stórauðigs	great-wealth
stórfé	great-wealth
stórmenni	great-men
stórœttaðr	great-family
strigadúk	sack-cloth
stumrar	stumbled
stund	awhile
stundlegum	temporary
stutt	short
styrk	support
suðr	south
sumar	summer
sumir	some
sumrinu	the-summer
svaf	slept
svara	answered
svarar	answered
Svarfaðardal	Svarfardal (place)
Svarfdœla	Svarfardal (place)
svarri	grave
Sveins	Svein (name)
svengd	hungry
sverð	a-sword
sverðinu	the-sword
Svíþjóð	Sweden (place)
svo	so
svöngum	hunger
sýnast	appear
sýndist	seemed-to
sýnduð	give-performance
syni	sons
Syrgisdölum	Syrgsdalir (place)
systr	sister
systra	sisters

T, t

Old Norse	English
taka	take, taken, took
talar	said

Word List (Old Norse to English)

Old Norse	English
talat	told
tekið	taken
tekr	take, took
tíðinda	news
tíðindi	news
tíðindum	news
til	for, the, to, until
tíma	time
tímir	time
togar	pulled
tók	received, took
töluðu	told
trautt	scarcely
trémann	wooden-man
tröllskap	witchcraft
tunguna	tongue
tvo	two
tvœr	two

Þ, þ

Old Norse	English
þá	then
þakkaði	thanked
þann	than, that, then
þar	them, there
þarf	needed
þarfa	needed
þarfaði	needed
þarfast	need
þarftu	need
þat	it, that, the, this, with
þau	they
þegar	straightaway, there
þeim	them, then, they
þeir	they
þeirra	theirs, there
þeirrar	there
þengils	the-prince
þenna	the, then, these, this, those
þér	to-you, you
þess	this
þessa	this
þessar	this
þessi	this
þessu	this
þessum	this
þetta	this
þig	you
þín	your
þingi	assembly
Þingvelli	Thingvellir (place)
þinn	you
þinna	yours
þinni	yours
þínum	yours
þitt	yours
þjóanna	thighs
þjóðskáld	skilled-poet
þjóin	thighs
þjónustumenn	servants
Þjórsá	Thjorsa (place)
þó	though
þökk	thanks
þoku	fog
Þokuvísr	Fog-verses (name)
þola	endure
þoldu	endured
Þórðar	Thord (name)
Þorgarð	Thorgard (name)
Þorgarði	Thorgard (name)
Þorgarðr	Thorgard (name), Thorgard (name)
Þorgarðs	Thorgard (name)
Þorgerði	Thorgerd (name)
Þórhildr	Thorhild (name)
Þorkell	Thorkell (name)
Þorleif	Thorleif (name)
Þorleifi	Thorleif (name), thorleif's
Þorleifr	Thorleif (name)
þorleifs	thorleif's, Thorleif's (name)
þorpara	peasant
þorsta	thirsty
þótti	thought
þóttist	thought
þóttu	thought
þóttust	thought
Þrándheim	Trondheim (place)
Þrasa	Thrasi (name)

Word List (Old Norse to English)

Old Norse	English
þriðjung	third
þrjá	three
Þrœnda	the-Tronds' (name)
þrotnum	waning
þú	you
þunga	heavy
þurfa	need
því	accordingly, because, since, such, then, therefore
þvílíkri	accordingly-like
þykir	seems, thought
þykist	thought
þykjast	considered
þykklega	arrogantly

U, u

Old Norse	English
um	about, at
umráða	about-advice
undan	back, out-of
undarlega	strange
undir	under, up-to
ungum	young
unni	loved
upp	up, upped
upphaf	beginning
uppi	up
urðu	became
utan	out, without
utarlega	out-lying

Ú, ú

Old Norse	English
úr	from, from-out-of, of, out, out-of
úrigr	unruly
út	out, out-from
útferð	funeral
úti	finished, out
útlendis	other-lands
útlœgr	outlaw

V, v

Old Norse	English
vaknar	awake, awoke
vald	power
valdi	controlled
valdið	caused
vanda	care
vandist	did
vandrœði	difficulty
vanr	experienced
var	was, were
varð	became, was, were
varla	scarcely
varning	wares
varninginn	wares
varpar	threw
vegsummerki	evidence, traces
veit	knows
veittu	granted
vel	well
veldr	brought-about
velli	the-fields
vellstœri	well-sized
vér	we
vera	be, becoming, being, be-it, to-be
verð	price
verða	become
verði	become, becomes
verðir	will-be
verðr	became, become
verðugu	honour
verðum	worth
verið	became, been, made
verki	work
verr	worst
vert	had-been
vesaldar	wretchedness
vestan	from-the-west, west
vestr	west
vestra	west
vetr	winter
vetra	winters
veturinn	winter
vexti	grown

Word List (Old Norse to English)

Old Norse	English	Old Norse	English
við	by, from, to, with	yðrum	yours
víða	widely	yfir	over
viðskiptis	behaved	yfirlœti	favour
vígdjarfr	slaying-warrior	yngsti	youngest
Vík	Vik (place)	Yngvildi	Yngvild (name)
víkinni	the-bay	ynni	win-over
vil	wish	yrði	became
vildi	wish, wished	yrkja	compose
vildir	wish	ytra	outside
viljið	will		
viljum	wish, wish-to		
villumaðr	villain		
víls	advantage		
vinsœl	popular		
vinsœldum	popularity		
virðingamaðr	man-of-high-rank		
virðingar	honour		
virðum	worthiness		
visku	wisdom		
vísr	verses		
víst	know		
vísu	certainly, this-verse, verse		
vísuna	verse		
vita	certainly, knew, know		
vitja	know		
vitr	wise		
vó	killed		
vœnna	good		
vœri	was, were		
völdum	doing		
völubrjótr	knuckle-breaker, knuckle-breaker		
von	hope		
vonda	wicked		
vor	spring		
vordögum	spring-days		
vori	the-spring		
vorið	spring, spring		
vort	ours		
voru	was, were		

Ý, ý

Old Norse	English
ýmist	either
ýtar	out

Y, y

Old Norse	English
yðr	you, yours

Word List *(English to Old Norse)*

English	Old Norse	English	Old Norse
A, a		appear	sýnast
		are	er, eru
a	at, eina, einn	are-you	ertu
about	á, at, í, um	a-ring	hring
about-advice	umráða	arranged	skipaði
abuse	níð	arrogantly	þykklega
accomplished-man	atgervimaðr	art	listar
accordingly	því	as	at, en, er, sem
accordingly-like	þvílíkri	as-a-beggar	stafkarls
actually	reyndar	a-second	annan
advantage	víls	Asgeir (name)	Ásgeir, Ásgeiri
adventure	œvintýr	a-ship	skip
advice	ráðum	ask	spyrja
after	áðr, aftr, eftir, síðan	asked	bat, beiddi, beiddist, biðr, spurði, spyr
after-the-case	eftirmáls	asks	spyr
afterwards	eftir, síðan	assembly	alþingi, þingi
age	aldr, aldri, elli, ellina	assistance	ásjá, fulltingi
a-great	mikils	a-sword	sverð
a-halberd	atgeir	at	á, at, í, um
a-little	lítillœti	ate	œti
all	alla, allan, allir, allri, alls, allt, öllu, öllum	Aud (name)	Auðr
		autumn	haustið
all-great	allmikill	avenge	hefna
allow	láta	awake	vakrar
also	og	away	brot, brott, burt
am	er	awhile	hríð, stund
am-able	nýtan	a-wife	konu
a-man	maðr	awoke	vaknar
a-mark	mörk	a-woman	kona
amnesia	óminnis		
ancestors	œtt	**B, b**	
ancestry	œtt		
ancient	fornum	back	aftr, undan
ancient-ways	fornfrœði, fornlegum	back-driven	afturreka
and	at, en, enda, og	bad	illa, illr
angry	œfr	badly	illa
another	annar	bag	hít
another's	annars	banquet	samsœtis
answered	svara, svarar	bargaining	kaupslagar
any	nokkuð	battle-fire	gunnelds
anything	nokkr	be	vera
a-poet	skáld		

41

Word List (English to Old Norse)

English	Old Norse
beard	skegg
became	urðu, varð, verðr, verið, yrði
because	því
become	orðið, verða, verði, verðr
becomes	verði
becoming	gerist, vera
been	verið
before	áðr, fyr, fyrir, fyrr
before him	fyrir
began	byrjaði, hóf
beggar	stafkarl
beggars	stafkarla, stafkarlar
beggar's	stafkarls
begin	hefja
beginning	upphaf
behaved	viðskiptis
being	sé, vera
be-it	vera
belonged	átt
belongings	góss
bench-fellows	bekkjunauta
better	batna, betr
bettered	batnaði
between	milli
bid	bat
blessed-life	sœllífi
blizzard	él
Blonduos (place)	Blönduósi
boats	báts
body	búkinn, líkama
boldly	skörulega
booth	búð, búðar
booths	búðanna
both	báðir, bœði
bought	kaupir, keypti
bound	binda, bindr
bowels	iðrin
brave	frœkni
break	brjótast
Brekka (place)	Brekku
bright	bjart
bring	fœra
broad-waist	miðdigr
brother	bróðr
brothers	brœðr, brœðrum
brought	fœra, fœrðu
brought-about	veldr
buried	heygðr
burned	brenna, brenndu
burnt	brenna
but	en, enn, og
by	við

C, c

English	Old Norse
call	heita, kalla
called	heitir, kalla, kallaðr, kölluðu
call-to	kalla
came	kemr, kom, koma, kominn, komst, komu
can	fœ, getr, kann
capable	gildr
care	gáir, vanda
cared	gáði
carried	báru, borið, bornir, fœrir
cast	kastaði
cattle	fé
caught	fengið, náði
caused	valdið
causing	framleiðslu
certainly	vísu, vita
character	gervi
chieftain	goði
chieftain-like	óhöfðinglegt
chieftains	höfðingja, höfðingjum
chieftains'	höfðingja
cleared	rœsta, ryðja, ryðr
clearly	glögglega
close	fast, nálœgt
closed	fast, lýkst
closely	fast
clothing	föt
coals	kolum
cold	köld, köldu, köldum
cold-bloodedly	kaldyrðum
combs	kömbum
come	kom, koma, komast

Word List (English to Old Norse)

English	Old Norse	English	Old Norse
comes	kemr, komi, kominn	*devil's*	fjandans
come-with	koma	*devious*	krókóttum
comfortable	hœgt	*did*	gerði, gerðu, vandist
coming	kominn	*died*	andaðr
commotion	háreysti	*difficulty*	vandrœði
companions	félaga, förunauta	*disappeared*	hvarf, steyptist
compose	yrkja	*disguise*	gervina
considered	þykjast	*disturbances*	óspekt
controlled	valdi	*doing*	völdum
could	gat, gœti, kom	*done*	búið, gera, gert
courageous-warrior	hildardjarfi	*doors*	dyrum
craft	iðn	*down*	niðr
created	smíða	*dragon*	naðrbings
crew	áhöfn, hásetum	*draw*	bregða
crutches	hœkjr	*drawn*	dregr
cunning	kyndugskap	*draws*	dregr
cursed	bölvaðra	*drew*	draga, hrukku
custom	háttum	*drift-wood*	rekabút
customers	kaupunauta, kaupunautar	*drink*	drykkju
		drinking-tables	drykkjuborð
		drive	reka
		drowned	drekktr
		dungeon	dýflissu

D, d

damage	skaða
dark	dökkri, myrkt
daughter	dóttir
day	dag
days	dögum
dead	bani, dauðu
dearest	dýrstum
death	andlát
decayed	rotnat
deceived	blekkir
decreased	minnkaði
decrepitude	örverpi
deeds	atgervi
deem	dœmt
delegates	fulltrúa
Denmark (place)	Danmerkr
descended	kynjaðr
descendents	œtt
desire	fýsi
desired	fýstist
desperation	örvœnt
destitution	andvana

E, e

each	hvergi, hverjum, hverri, hvert, hvorri
earl	jarl, jarli
Earl-Of-Lade (name)	Hlaðajarl, Hlaðajarls
earls	jarls
earl's-abuse	jarlsníðs
Earl's-Poet (name)	Jarlaskáld
early-age	snemma
east	austr
eat	át, eta
eighteen	átján
either	eða, ýmist
either-way	annaðhvort
eldest	elst
elephant	fíl
end	enda, lokið
ends	lýkr
endure	þola
endured	þoldu

Word List (English to Old Norse)

English	Old Norse	*English*	Old Norse
England (place)	Englandi	*food*	góða, kost, leiðarnests, matar
enslavement	ánauð	*for*	á, at, fyrir, í, til
equally	jafnan	*forests*	skógum
equipped	gyrti	*for-good*	alfari
equipped-with	gyrðr	*for-himself*	sér
Erik's (name)	Eiríks	*for-long*	lengr
errand	erindis	*for-the-sake*	sakir
estate	óðali	*forty*	fertuga
evening	kveldið	*forward*	fram
events	atburð, atburðir	*foster-care*	ástfóstr
evidence	vegsummerki	*fostered*	fóstri
evil	illu	*foster-father*	fóstra
evil-like	illslegr	*found*	fann, finnr
exceedingly-much	geysimjǫk	*from*	á, af, at, er, frá, fram, í, úr, við
excellent-man	íþróttamaðr	*from-out-of*	úr
except	nema	*from-the-west*	vestan
exchanged	skipti	*from-told*	frásagnar
experienced	vanr	*full*	fullu
Eyjafjoll-Mountains (place)	Eyjafjöllum	*full-coming*	fullkomið
		funeral	útferð

F, f

G, g

English	Old Norse	*English*	Old Norse
fair	sœmilega	*Gaseyri (place)*	Gáseyri
Fair-Cheek (name)	Fagurkinn	*gave*	gaf, gáfu
fair-wind	byrjar	*generosity*	örleik
fame	frœgt, orðstír	*get*	fá, fást, fœ, geta, getr
farm	búi	*ghastly*	ljótu
farmer	bónda	*gifted*	lánat
father	faðir, föðr	*gifts*	gjafir
favour	yfirlœti	*give*	gefa
fee-lot	fjárhlut	*give-performance*	sýnduð
fell	féll, fellr, féllu	*gladly*	gjarna
financial-loss	fjártjón	*go*	ganga
financial-share	fjárhlut	*goat-beard*	geitarskegg, geitarskegginu
find	fund	*God (name)*	Guðs
finished	úti	*going*	farið, gengr
first	fyrst	*gone*	farið, gengið
first-mate	háseta	*good*	góðan, góðar, góðu, gott, vœnna
fog	þoku	*got*	fékk, fengi, fengið, gat, gekk, gœti
Fog-verses (name)	Þokuvísr	*got-married*	kvœntist
followed	fylgdi, fylgt		
following	afliðið		
following-men	fjölmenni		

Word List (English to Old Norse)

English	Old Norse	English	Old Norse
granted	veittu	heaven's	himins
grave	svarri	heavy	þunga
great	mikill	he-had	honum
great-family	stórœttaðr	he-himself	sér
great-men	stórmenni	Hel (place)	Helju
great-wealth	stórauðigs, stórfé	held	hélt
greeted	kvaddi	Helgi (name)	Helgi
greeting	kvaðningar	hellish-old-man	heljarkarl
grips	festist	here	hér, hingat
grown	vexti	hers	hennar
		high	hátt

H, h

English	Old Norse	English	Old Norse
		high-born	ítri
		him	hann, honum, sér, sig
had	á, átt, áttu, hafa, hafði, hefir, hefr, lagði, láta, láti, lét, lœtr, œti	himself	sé, sér, sína, sinni
		hired	rœðr
		his	hans, hánum, hins, honum, sér, sína, sinn, sinna, sinnar, sinni, síns, sínu, sínum, sitt
had-been	vert		
had-done	gerði		
hair	hárið	Hofdabrekka (place)	Höfðabrekku
Hakon (name)	Hákon, Hákonar	hold	halda
Hakon's (name)	Hákonar	home	heim
halberd	atgeirnum	homes	heim
half	hálf	honour	sœmd, verðugu, virðingar
Hali (name)	Hali		
Hallbjorn (name)	Hallbirni, Hallbjörn	hope	von
hands	hendi	Horgabrudi (name)	Hörgabrúði
hanged	hengja	Horgi (place)	Hörgi
happened	gerðist	however	hversu
hardly	harðla	how-so	hversu
harm	skaði	humiliation	smánar
harmful	dálegra	humility	lítillœt
harsher	harðúðigr	hunger	svörgum
has	er, hefir	hungry	svergd
hated	hataðr		
have	fá, hafa, hafi, hafið, haft, hefi, hefir, höfum, lagið		

I, i

English	Old Norse
having	hefir
he	hann, hans, honum, sér
i	eg
i-am	mér
Iceland (place)	Ísland, Íslandi, Íslands
head-skin	höfuðsvörðum
idol-worship	guðníðingskapr
hear	heyrið
if	ef, eg
heard	heyrði, heyrðu, heyrt
ill	illa, illr
heart	hjartat, hugr
improvement	góðu

Word List (English to Old Norse)

English	Old Norse
in	á, af, at, í, inn
increase	aukið
in-front-of	framan
inherited	erfðu
instruction	frœðum
intended	œtlaði
into	í
invited	bat, boðið
iron-weapon	járn
Irpu (name)	Irpu
is	er
is-said	segja
it	á, at, hana, hún, þat
itching	kláði
it-is	er
its	hennar
it-was	gerði

J, j

English	Old Norse
journey	ferðum, leið
Jutland (place)	Jóta

K, k

English	Old Norse
Karl (name)	Karl
kennings	kenningar
kill	drepa
killed	vó
king's-gift	konungsnaut
kinsmen	frœnda
kinsmen-origins	kynferði
Klaufi (name)	Klaufa
knew	kunni, vita
knots	knúta
know	kannt, víst, vita, vitja
known	kenndr
knows	veit
knuckle-breaker	völubrjótr, völubrjótr

L, l

English	Old Norse
Lade (place)	Hlaðir, Hlöðum
laid	lagði, lagið, lét, liggr
land	land
lands	lands
large	mikill, stóra
last	síðasta
laughed	hlógu
launched	skjóta
law-assembly	lögréttu
lay	liggr
laying	legið
leading	skörungr
learned	spurði, spurn, spurt, spyr
leave	orlof
left	lœtr
legislation	lagasetning
lengthen	lengja
less	síðr
let	lát, látið, lét
levelled	sléttri
lies	liggr
life	líf
life-days	lífsdaga
lifetime	lífstíma
like	líkar
liked	líkaði
liking	geðjast
listen	hlýða
listen-to	hlýdduð
little	lítils, lítinn
lived	bjó
Ljotolf (name)	Ljótólfi, Ljótólfr, Ljótólfs
locks	lásum
long	lengi
longer	lengr, lengra
lord	herra
lordship	höfðingskap
loved	unni
luck	giftu

M, m

English	Old Norse
made	ger, gera, gerðu, verið
magic	fítonsanda

Word List (English to Old Norse)

English	Old Norse
magical-arts	göldrum
malice	grálega
malignance	meinlœtum
malignancy	meinlœtis
man	karli, maðr, mann
man-evil	mannillska
man-of-high-rank	virðingamaðr
man's	manna
manslaughter	mannalát
many	marga, margan, margir, margra, margri, mart, mörg, mörgum
many-known	margkunnandi
market-town	kaupstaðinn
marshes	mörkum
matter	mál
may	má, mátti, mega, megi
me	mér, mig
meet	fund
men	drengr, manna, menn, mönnum
merchant-ships	knarrar
merry	œrnri
met	hitti
middle	miðjum, miðs
middle-of	miðju
Midfjord (place)	Miðfirði
Midfjorder-Skeggi (name)	Miðfjarðar-Skeggja
midwinter-evening	aðfangskveld
mile	mílu
mine	minn, mitt
misery	eymd
misliked	mislíkaði
miss	missa
moment	bili
money	peninga
more	fleira, meir, meira
more-convenient	hentugri
morning	morguninn
most	flestum, mest, mesta, mesti, mikið
mother	móðr
mother's-brother	móðrbróðr
mound	haug, haugr
mouth	munn
move	flyttu
moved	garg
movement	bragði
much	margra, mikið, mikil, mikill, mikils, mikinn, mikla, miklar, miklum, mjǫk
must	mun
Myrdal-Valley (place)	Mýdal
mysterious-path	refilstiga

N, n

English	Old Norse
name	heiti, nafn, nafni
named	heita, heiti, heitir, hét
name-giving	nafnfesti
nature	eðli, náttúra
near	nœr
nearest	nœstir
need	þarfast, þarftu, þurfa
needed	þarf, þarfa, þarfaði
never	aldrei
news	tíðinda, tíðindi, tíðindum
next	nœsta
Nidung (name)	Níðungr
night	nátt, nœtr
nineteen	nítján
Njord (name)	Njörðr
noble	öðlings, skörungr
noble-woman	kvenskörungr
noise	hark
no-little	ólítið
none	engi, engr, önga
nor	né
north	norðr
Norway (place)	Noreg, Noregs
not	eiga, eigi, ekki, öngu
not-further	áfram
not-lacking	óvant
now	nú

Word List (English to Old Norse)

English	Old Norse	*English*	Old Norse

O, o

English	Old Norse
Odin (name)	Gautr
of	á, af, at, í, og, úr
of-all	öllum
off	af
of-gold	gulls
of-Hakon	hákoni
of-poets	skálda
often	oft, oftar, oftlega
of-the-ship	knarrar
Olaf (name)	Ólafr
Olaf's (name)	Ólafs
old	gamall, gamla, gömlum
old-man	gamlir, karl
omens	frétt, fréttar
on	á
one	eina, einn
one's	hvern
only	einna
open	opnast
opening	gíman
or	eða, ella
other	aðrar, aðrir, annar, annarra, annarri, hinum, öðrum
other-lands	útlendis
others	aðrir, annarra, öðrum
ours	vort
ourselves-decide	sjálfráða
out	úr, út, utan, úti, ýtar
out-from	út
outlaw	útlœgr
out-lying	utarlega
out-of	undan, úr
outside	ytra
over	ofan, yfir
own	eigið
owning	eign
Oxara (place)	Öxará

P, p

English	Old Norse
parted	skildu
parting	reikar
passage	farning
passed	leið
peasant	þorpara
people	manna, manni, manninn, menn, mönnum
peoples'	mönnum
performed	flutt
pernickety	nákvœmi
phrases	drápu
plates	diska
plunder	férán
plundering	hervirki
poem	kveðið, kvœði, kvœðið
poems	kvœði
poem's-reward	kvœðislaunum
poet	skáld
poetry	brag, skáldskap, skáldskapinn
poles	ásum
popular	vinsœl
popularity	vinsœldum
possible	hœgt
power	krafti, mögnuðu, vald
powerful	ríkr
praise	lof
praised	lofaði
praise-words	lofkvœði
prepared	bjó, búinn, býr
previous-deeds	framaverka
price	verð
profit	grœddi
promise	heita
promised	hét
promising	efnilegir
promptly	greiðlega
properly	sœmilega
proverb	orðskvið
provide	kost
provided-knowing	naddveiti

Word List (English to Old Norse)

English	Old Norse
pulled	togar
punishment-time	hegningartíminn
put-to-words	kveðið

Q, q

quickly	bráðlega, greiðlega

R, r

English	Old Norse
ran	hleypr
rather	heldr
received	tók
recently	litlu
recites	kveða
recovered	raknaði
Red (name)	Rauði
Red-Cloak (name)	Rauðfeldr
reddened	roðið
relief	létti
relieved	fegins
renown	hróðr
repaid	galt
repay	gjalda, launat
repayment	gjöld
reported	fréttust
requirements	hentar
rest	hvílast
restlessness	óvœra, óvœri
return	áðr
returned	aftr
returning	aftr
revenge	hefnda
Reykir (place)	Reykjum
river	á
robbed	rœndi
robbery	ránum
rocks	grjóti
rose	ríða, rís
rough	harðleikinn
ruled	réð

S, s

English	Old Norse
sack-cloth	strigadúk
sacrifices	fórnir
saga	sögu
sagas	sögr
said	kvat, kveðr, mœlt, sagði, sagðr, sagt, segið, segir, segja, sögðu, talar
sailed	siglou
sake	sakir, sœkja
sale	sölr
same	sömu
sand	eyri
sat	sat, sest
saw	sá, sér, sjá
say	kveða, segist, segja
say-you	segðu
scarcely	trautt, varla
scratched	hrífa
sea	haf
secrecy	laun
see	sé, sjá
seemed-to	sýndist
seems	þykir
seen	sést
sent	sendu
servants	þjónustumenn
settled	bjó, búið
settlement	byggða
shall	mun, munt, munuð, munum, skal, skalt, skaltu
shall-i	mig
shall-you	skaltu
shame	blygðar, skammar
shamed	forsmáðr
shaped	skapaðir
she	hún
shepherd	sauðamaðr
ship	skip, skipi, skips
ships	skips
shivering	hrollir
short	stutt

Word List (English to Old Norse)

English	Old Norse	English	Old Norse
should	mun, munuð, skyldi, skyldr, skyldu	stave	stef
shoulders	herðar	staves	stafni
show-off	skruma	sticks	stafina
shut	luktum	stood	standa, stendr, stóð
side	megin	stopped	linnir
since	síðan, því	stories	saga
sister	systr	straightaway	þegar
sisters	systra	strange	kynstrum, undarlega
sit	sœti, sœtis	strangeness	býsn
sit-still	kyrr	strong	gilds
Skeggi (name)	Skeggi, Skeggja	struck	hjó
skilled	íþrótt, íþróttir	stumbled	stumrar
skilled-in-magic	fjölkunni	such	slíkt, því
skilled-poet	þjóðskáld	summer	sumar
skills	íþrótta	support	styrk
Skogar (place)	Skógum	supposed	œtluðu
slaying-warrior	vígdjarfr	Svarfardal (place)	Svarfaðardal, Svarfdœla
slendered	grenndi	Svein (name)	Sveins
slept	sofnar, svaf	swagger	skruma
slyness	slœgða	Sweden (place)	Svíþjóð
so	sá, svo	swords	branda
soles-of-the-feet	iljarnar	Syrgsdalir (place)	Syrgisdölum
solve	leysa		
some	nokkuð, nokkura, nokkurar, nokkurt, sumir		

T, t

English	Old Norse
something	nokkuð
somewhat	nokkuð
son	son, sonar	take	náms, numið, taka, tekr
songs	atkvœðum	taken	nema, taka, tekið
son-of-gjallandi	gjallandason	talented	gervilegr
sons	syni	talked	mœlti
soon	fljótlega	teach	kenna
soonest	fljótasta	temple	hofi
sorcery	galdr	temples	hof
sought	fréttist, leitaði, sótt	temporary	stundlegum
soul	andar	than	en, þann
south	suðr	thanked	þakkaði
speak	kveða	thanks	þökk
spikes	broddr	that	á, at, en, er, sem, þann, þat
spoke	kvat, mœlti	the	at, en, er, hið, hinn, hinni, hins, hinu, þat, þenna, til
spoken	kveðið		
spring	vor, vorið, vorið		
spring-days	vordögum	the-abuse	níðið
stand	staðið, standa	the-bag	hítina

50

Word List (English to Old Norse)

English	Old Norse	English	Old Norse
the-bay	víkinni	the-tables	borð
the-best	mest, mesta	the-Tronds' (name)	Þrœnda
the-chieftain	goða	the-uppermost	ofanverðum
the-coals	kol	they	þau, þeim, þeir
the-crutches	hœkjurnar	they-were	eru
the-darkness	myrkrið	thick-clouds	mökkr
the-day	daginn	thighs	þjóanna, þjóin
the-earl	jarl, jarli, jarlinn, jarlinum, jarls	Thingvellir (place)	Þingvelli
		think	hugsa
the-earl's	jarls	third	þriðjung
the-earl's-abuse	jarlsníði	thirsty	þorsta
the-earth	jörðina	this	á, at, þat, þenna, þess, þessa, þessar, þessi, þessu, þessum, þetta
the-enemy's	óvinarins		
the-fellows	drengjum		
the-fields	velli		
the-greatest	mestr	this-verse	vísu
the-hall	höllina, höllinni	Thjorsa (place)	Þjórsá
theirs	sinn, þeirra	Thord (name)	Þórðar
the-king	konung, konungi, konungr, konungs	Thorgard (name)	Þorgarð, Þorgarði, Þorgarðr, Þorgarðr, Þorgarðs
the-land	land, landi		
the-lion's	leóns	Thorgerd (name)	Þorgerði
them	þar, þeim	Thorhild (name)	Þórhildr
the-mauler	böggva	Thorkell (name)	Þorkell
the-most	flestu	Thorleif (name)	Þorleif, Þorleifi, Þorleifr
the-mound	hauginn, hauginum, haugurinn		
		thorleif's	þorleifi, þorleifs
the-mound-dweller	haugbúann	Thorleif's (name)	Þorleifs
then	at, en, hið, hina, þá, þann, þeim, þenna, því	those	hinn, þenna
		though	þó
		thought	þótti, þóttist, þóttu, þóttust, þykir, þykist
the-night	nóttina		
the-old-man	karl, karli	thoughts	hug
the-poem	kvœðið	Thrasi (name)	Þrasa
the-poet	skaldi	three	þrjá
the-prince	þengils	threw	varpar
there	þar, þegar, þeirra, þeirrar	through	gegnum
		tied-up	binda
therefore	því	time	tíma, tímir
the-same	samr	to	á, at, í, til, við
these	þenna	to-be	vera
the-ship	nökkvi, skipið	to-carry	flytja
the-spring	vori	to-eat	etið
the-straw	hálminn	together	saman
the-summer	sumrinu	to-give	gefa
the-sword	sverðinu	to-hear	hlýða

Word List (English to Old Norse)

English	Old Norse
to-him	honum, sér
told	sagði, talat, töluðu
told-of	getið
to-me	mér
tongue	tunguna
took	nam, taka, tekr, tók
torment	kvala
to-sell	selja
tough	seigt
toughness	harðfengi
to-you	þér
traces	vegsummerki
trading-men	kaupmönnum
traditions	sið
transport	reiða
travel	fara, ferð, ferðar
travel-goods	fararefna
travelled	farið, fer, fór, fóru
tricked	bregðr, ginnti
Trondheim (place)	Þrándheim
troubled	bœginn
truly	sannlega
tunic	kyrtilinn, kyrtlinum
turned	hverfr, snýr, snýst
twisted	snaraði
two	tvo, tvœr
true	satt

U, u

English	Old Norse
unconsciousness	óvit
under	undir
undone	ógert, óloknum
un-eagerly	ófreklegar
un-glad	ógleðr
un-gladdened	ógladdist
un-gladness	ógleði
unknown	ókunna
unless	nema
un-redeemable	óbœtilegs
unruly	úrigr
unsoundly	óhljóði
until	til
up	upp, uppi
upped	upp
upper	efsta
up-to	undir
us	oss
usually	jafnan

V, v

English	Old Norse
vacations	orlofs
verse	vísu, vísuna
verses	vísr
Vik (place)	Vík
villain	villumaðr
vocabulary	orðfœri

W, w

English	Old Norse
walked	gekk
waning	þrotnum
wares	varning, varninginn
warrior	gramr
warriors	fyrðum
was	enn, er, var, varð, vœri, voru
was-named	hét, nefndist
wave	öldu
we	oss, vér
wealth	fé
wealth-damage	fjárskaða
wealthy	auðigr
we-are	eru
well	vel
well-sized	vellstœri
went	fékk, fer, fór, fóru, ganga,ганganda, gekk, gengr
were	var, varð, vœri, voru
west	vestan, vestr, vestra
what	er, hvat, sem
wheel	röðla
when	en, er
whether	hvort
which	er, sem
who	er, hver
who's	hverjum

Word List (English to Old Norse)

English	Old Norse	English	Old Norse
who-was	er	yule-feast	jólaveislunnar
why	hví		
wicked	vonda		
widely	víða		
wife	kona		
will	viljið		
will-be	verðir		
willingly	ofléttlega		
win-over	ynni		
winter	vetr, veturinn		
winters	vetra		
wisdom	visku		
wise	vitr		
wish	vil, vildi, vildir, viljum		
wished	vildi		
wish-to	viljum		
witchcraft	fjölkynngi, gerningum, tröllskap		
with	í, með, þat, við		
with-conviction	sakir		
without	án, utan		
woman	kona		
Woman-Verses (name)	Konrvísr		
wooden-man	trémann		
worded	ort		
words	orð, orðið, ort, orti		
work	verki		
worst	verr		
worth	verðum		
worthiness	virðum		
would	mundi, mundu		
wretchedness	vesaldar		
written	rituð		

Y, y

English	Old Norse
Yngvild (name)	Yngvildi
you	þér, þig, þinn, þú, yðr
young	ungum
youngest	yngsti
your	þín
yours	þinna, þinni, þínum, þitt, yðr, yðrum
Yule (name)	Jóla

The Tale of Thorlief the Earl's Poet (*Old Icelandic*)

Old Icelandic	Literal	English
1	**1**	**1**
Nú skal segja þann ævintýr er gerðist á ofanverðum dögum Hákonar Hlaðajarls, í hverjum kynstrum, göldrum og gerningum hann varð forsmáður og mjög að verðugu, því að hans mannillska og guðníðingskapur varð mörgum manni til mikils þunga og óbætilegs skaða andar og líkama.	Now shall say then adventure that happened in the-uppermost days Hakon Earl-Of-Lade, about who's strange, magical-arts and witchcraft he was shamed and much to honour, because that he man-evil and idol-worship became many people to much heavy and un-redeemable damage soul and body.	Now shall be told the adventure that happened in the early days of Hakon the earl of Lade, about his strange magic and witchcraft which greatly shamed his honour, because this evil man and his idolatry became a heavy burden to many people, and caused irreparable harm to soul and body.
Varð honum það sem margan tímir að þá er hegningartíminn er kominn er eigi hægt undan að komast því að það er óvinarins náttúra að þann manninn sem hann þykist fullkomið vald á eiga og önga von á til guðs blekkir hann fyrst og blygðar með krókóttum kyndugskap sinna bölvaðra slægða í framleiðslu hans ljótu lífsdaga en að þrotnum hans stundlegum lífstíma verður hann drekktur í dökkri dýflissu dálegra kvala með eymd og ánauð utan enda.	Became to-him that as many time that then was punishment-time was came that not possible out-of to come because that it was the-enemy's nature that then people which he thought full-coming power that not and none hope of to God deceived he first and shame with devious cunning his cursed slyness in causing his ghastly life-days then that waning his temporary lifetime became he drowned in dark dungeon harmful torment with misery and enslavement without end.	It befell him, as it does to many, when the time of punishment came, he could not come out of it, as it was the devil's nature to deceive people who he thinks he has full power over, and who has no hope of God's mercy. First comes shame with devious cunning and cursed slyness, causing a ghastly life, and in the waning of his temporary life, he is drowned in the dark dungeon of harmful torment, with misery and enslavement without end.
2	**2**	**2**
Þá bjó Ásgeir rauðfeldur á Brekku í Svarfaðardal.	Then lived Asgeir Red-Cloak at Brekka in Svarfardal.	Then Asgeir Red-Cloak lived at Brekka in Svafardal.
Hann var ríkur maður og stórættaður.	He was powerful man and great-family.	He was a powerful man from a great family.
Þórhildur hét kona hans.	Thorhild named wife his.	His wife was named Thorhild.
Hún var vitur kona og vinsæl og skörungur mikill.	She was wise woman and popular and noble much.	She was a very wise, popular, and noble woman.

The Tale of Thorlief the Earl's Poet (Old Icelandic)

Old Icelandic	Literal	English
Þau áttu þrjá syni og voru allir efnilegir.	They had three sons and were all promising.	They had three sons, all of whom were promising.
Ólafur hét son þeirra hinn elsti og var kallaður völubrjótur, annar Helgi hinn frækni og koma þeir báðir meir við aðrar sögur en þessa.	Olaf named son theirs the eldest and was called knuckle-breaker, another Helgi the brave and came they both more with other sagas than this.	Their eldest son was named Olaf, who was called 'knuckle-breaker', the second son was called Helgi the brave, and they appear in other sagas than this one.
Þorleifur hét hinn yngsti son þeirra.	Thorleif named the youngest son theirs.	Their youngest son was named Thorleif.
Hann var snemma gildur og gervilegur og hinn mesti atgervimaður um íþróttir.	He was early-age capable and talented and the most accomplished-man at skilled.	He was fully capable at an early age, an accomplished man and skilful.
Hann var skáld gott.	He was a-poet good.	He was a good poet
Hann var á fóstri með Miðfjarðar-Skeggja móðurbróður sínum að Reykjum í Miðfirði þar til er hann var átján vetra gamall.	He was in fostered with Midfjorder-Skeggi mother's-brother his at Reykir in Midfjord there until that he was eighteen winters old.	He was brought up with his uncle Midfjorder-Skeggi at Reykir in Midfjord there until he was eighteen years old.
Skeggi unni mikið Þorleifi og lagði við hann ástfóstur.	Skeggi loved much Thorleif and had with him foster-care.	Skeggi loved Thorleif very much and brought him up with care.
Það töluðu menn að Skeggi mundi fleira kenna Þorleifi í fræðum fornlegum en aðrir mundu vita.	This told people that Skeggi would more teach Thorleif in instruction ancient-ways than others would know.	People said that Skeggi would teach Thorleif more about the ways of magic than others would know.
Þá fór Þorleifur heim til föður síns.	Then went Thorleif home to father his.	Then Thorleif went home to his father.
Hann vó Klaufa böggva með fulltingi Ólafs bróður síns en til eftirmáls eftir Klaufa var Karl hinn rauði og gekk svo fast að að Þorleifur varð útlægur og ger í burt úr Svarfaðardal.	He killed Klaufi the-mauler with assistance Olaf's brother his and to after-the-case after Klaufi was Karl the Red and went so closed it that Thorleif became outlaw and made to away from-out-of Svarfardal.	He killed Klaufi the mauler with the help of his brother Olaf, and in the following legal case was Karl the Red, and so it concluded that Thorleif became an outlaw and banished from Svafardal.
Ljótólfur goði hafði fylgt Yngvildi fagurkinn systur Þorleifs.	Ljotolf chieftain had followed Yngvild Fair-Cheek sister Thorleif's.	Ljotolf the chieftain lived with Yngvild the fair-cheek, Thorleif's sister.

The Tale of Thorlief the Earl's Poet (Old Icelandic)

Old Icelandic	Literal	English
Hann kom Þorleifi í skip á Gáseyri.	He came Thorleif to ship at Gaseyri.	He brought Thorleif to a ship at Gaseyri.
Þorleifur varð afturreka.	Thorleif became back-driven.	But Thorleif was driven back.
Hann var um veturinn á laun ýmist með Ljótólfi goða eða Ásgeiri föður sínum.	He was about winter in secrecy either with Ljotolf the-chieftain or Asgeir father his.	During the winter he was hiding with Ljotolf the chieftain or his father Asgeir.
Nam hann þá að föður sínum marga fornfræði því að hann var sagður margkunnandi.	Took he then to father his many ancient-ways because that he was said many-known.	He then took to learning many of the ancient ways, as it is said that he knew many things.
Var þá Þorleifur nítján vetra.	Was then Thorleif nineteen winters.	Thorleif was then nineteen winters old.
Karl leitaði fast eftir um Þorleif og urðu þar um veturinn margir atburðir, þeir er frásagnar eru verðir sem segir í Svarfdæla sögu.	Karl sought closely after about Thorleif and became there about winter many events, they are from-told are will-be as said in Svarfardal saga.	Karl looked closely for Thorleif, and from there came many events, which are told in Svafardal Saga.
Um vorið eftir fór Þorleifur vestur til Skeggja fóstra síns og frænda og biður hann ásjá og umráða með sér um þessi mál.	About spring after travelled Thorleif west to Skeggi foster-father his and kinsmen and asked him assistance and about-advice with him about this matter.	About the following spring, Thorleif travelled west to Skeggi his foster father and kinsman, and asked for his help and guidance in this matter.
Og með styrk og ráðum Miðfjarðar-Skeggja og Ljótólfs goða fer Þorleifur og kaupir sér skip að kaupmönnum er uppi stóð í Blönduósi og ræður háseta til og fór síðan heim á Brekku og hitti föður sinn og móður og beiddist af þeim fararefna og fékk svo mikinn fjárhlut sem honum þótti sér þarfa og að vordögum lét hann varning sinn til skips binda og fór í brott af Brekku alfari og bað vel fyrir föður sínum og móður og Miðfjarðar-Skeggja fóstra sínum.	And with support and advice Midfjorder-Skeggi and Ljotolf the-chieftain went Thorleif and bought himself a-ship from trading-men that up stood in Blonduos and hired first-mate for and travelled afterwards home to Brekka and met father his and mother and asked of them travel-goods and got so much fee-lot as he thought he-himself needed and to spring-days had he wares his to ship bound and travelled to away from Brekka for-good and bid well for father his and mother and Midfjorder-Skeggi foster-father his.	And with the support and advice of Midfjorder-Skeggi and Ljotolf the chieftain, Thorleif went and bought himself a ship from merchants up in Blonduos, and hired a first mate for it. After that he then travelled home to Brekka and met his father and mother, asking for wares and travel goods, and he got as much money as he thought he needed. In the first days of spring he brought his wares to his ship, bound them up, and travelled away from Brekka once and for all, wishing his father and mother well, and Midfjorder-Skeggi, his foster father.

The Tale of Thorlief the Earl's Poet (Old Icelandic)

Old Icelandic	Literal	English
# 3	# 3	# 3
Nú lætur Þorleifur í haf og byrjar honum vel og kemur skipi sínu í Vík austur.	Now left Thorleif to sea and fair-wind he-had well and came ship his into Vik east.	Now Thorleif set out to sea and got a fair wind, and his ship came to Vik in the east.
Hákon Hlaðajarl var þá í Víkinni.	Hakon Earl-Of-Lade was then in The-bay.	Hakon was the earl of Lade at Vik.
Þorleifur gekk á land og lét ryðja skip sitt.	Thorleif went to the-land and had cleared ship his.	Thorleif went to land and had is ship unloaded.
Hann hitti jarlinn og kvaddi hann.	He met the-earl and greeted him.	He met the earl and greeted him.
Jarl tók honum vel og spurði hann að nafni, ætt og kynferði en Þorleifur sagði honum.	The-earl received him well and asked him of name, ancestors and kinsmen-origins and Thorleif told him.	The earl received him well and asked his name, ancestry, and origins, and Thorleif told him.
Jarl spurði og margra tíðinda af Íslandi en Þorleifur sagði honum ofléttlega.	The-earl asked of much news of Iceland and Thorleif told him willingly.	The earl asked for much news of Iceland, and Thorleif told him.
Þá sagði jarl:	Then said the-earl:	Then the earl said:
"Svo er orðið Þorleifur að vér viljum hafa sölur af þér og hásetum þínum".	"So has become Thorleif that we wish-to have sale of you and crew yours".	"So it is, Thorleif, that we wish to buy some things from you and your crew".
Þorleifur svarar:	Thorleif answered:	Thorleif answered:
"Vér höfum lítinn varninginn herra en oss eru þó aðrir kaupunautar hentugri og munuð þér láta oss sjálfráða vera að selja þeim góss vort og peninga sem oss líkar".	"We have little wares lord and us we-are though other customers more-convenient and shall you allow us ourselves-decide being for to-sell them belongings ours and money as we like".	"We have little in the way of wares, my lord, and we need more useful customers, and you shall allow us to decide for ourselves who to sell our belongings to as we like".
Jarli þótti hann þykklega svara og mislíkaði orð hans mjög og skildu við svo búið.	Earl thought he arrogantly answered and misliked words his much and parted with so settled.	The earl thought he had answered arrogantly, and disliked his words, and with that they parted.

The Tale of Thorlief the Earl's Poet (Old Icelandic)

Old Icelandic	Literal	English
Þorleifur fór nú til manna sinna og svaf af um nóttina og um morguninn rís hann upp og fer í kaupstaðinn og fréttist fyrir um góða kaupunauta og kaupslagar við þá um daginn.	Thorleif travelled now to men his and slept of about the-night and about morning rose he up and travelled to market-town and sought for about food customers and bargaining with then about the-day.	Thorleif went back to his men and slept through the night, and in the morning he got up and travelled to town and sought good customers, and bargained with them throughout the day.
Og er jarl spurði það fór hann með fjölmenni til skips Þorleifs og lét taka þar menn alla og binda.	And when the-earl learned that travelled he with following-men to ships Thorleif's and had took there men all and tied-up.	And when the earl learned of this, he travelled with his followers to Thorleif's ship and took all the men and had them tied up.
Síðan rændi hann þar fjárhlut öllum og kastaði á sinni eign en lét brenna skipið að köldum kolum.	Afterwards robbed he there financial-share of-all and cast about himself owning and had burnt the-ship to cold coals.	Afterwards he robbed them of all their wealth and took it for himself, and had the ship burnt to coals.
Og eftir þetta lét hann skjóta ásum milli búðanna og lét þar hengja við alla förunauta Þorleifs.	And after this had he launched poles between booths and had them hanged with all companions Thorleif's.	After this he had poles raised between booths and had all of Thorleif's companions hanged.
Síðan fór jarl í brott og hans menn og tók að sér varning þann er Þorleifur hafði átt og skipti upp með sínum mönnum.	Afterwards travelled the-earl to away and his men and took then for-himself wares then that Thorleif had had and exchanged up with his men.	Afterwards the earl went away with his men, taking all the wares and dividing it among his men.
En um kveldið er Þorleifur kom heim og ætlaði að vitja manna sinna sem hann gerði sá hann vegsummerki hversu við hans félaga hafði farið verið og þóttist vita að Hákon jarl mundi þessu vonda verki valdið hafa og spyr nú eftir þessum tíðindum glögglega.	Then about evening when Thorleif came home and intended to know men his what he had-done saw he traces how-so with his companions had gone been and thought certainly that Hakon earl would this wicked work caused had and learned now after this news clearly.	In the evening when Thorleif came home and looked for his men as usual, he saw traces of what had happened with his companions, and thought certainly that Earl Hakon caused this evil deed, and afterwards he learned the full news clearly.
Og er hann hafði þessi tíðindi sannlega spurt þá kvað hann vísu:	And when he had this news truly learned then spoke he this-verse:	And when he learned the news, then he spoke this verse:
Hrollir hugr minn illa. Hefir drengr skaða fengið sé eg á sléttri eyri, svarri, báts og knarrar.	Shivering heart mine badly. Have men damage caught see i this levelled sand, grave, boats and merchant-ships.	My heart shivers badly. Men have caught damage, I see this levelled sand, grave, both ship and boat.

The Tale of Thorlief the Earl's Poet (Old Icelandic)

Old Icelandic	Literal	English
Hinn er upp réð brenna öldu fíl fyrir skaldi, hver veit nema kol knarrar köld fýsi mig gjalda.	Those are up ruled burned wave elephant before the-poet, who knows except the-coals of-the-ship cold desire shall-i repay.	Those that ruled to burn the elephant of the waves, who knows except the coals of the ship cold desire I to repay.

4

Svo er sagt að eftir þenna atburð kom Þorleifur sér í skip með kaupmönnum og sigldu suður til Danmerkur og fór hann á fund Sveins konungs og var með honum um veturinn.	So it-is said that after those events came Thorleif himself in a-ship with trading-men and sailed south to Denmark and travelled he to meet Svein the-king and was with him about winter.	It is said that after this Thorleif went on a ship with trading-men and sailed south to Denmark, and he travelled to meet king Svein and stayed with him over the winter.
En er hann hafði þar eigi lengi verið var það einn dag að Þorleifur gekk fyrir konung og beiddi hann hlýða kvæði því er hann hafði ort um hann.	Then when he had there not long been was it one day that Thorleif went before the-king and asked him to-hear poem since that he had worded about him.	Then when he had not long been there, one day Thorleif went before the king and asked hi to hear a poem that he had composed about him.
Konungur spurði hvort hann væri skáld.	The-king asked whether he was a-poet.	The king asked whether he was a poet.
Þorleifur svarar:	Thorleif answered:	Thorleif answered:
"Það er eftir því sem þér viljið dæmt hafa herra er þér heyrið".	"It is after therefore which to-you will deem have lord when you hear".	"That is for you to judge, lord, when you have heard it".
Konungur bað hann þá fram flytja.	The-king asked him then from to-carry.	The king then asked him to perform.
Þorleifur kvað þá fertuga drápu og er þetta stef í:	Thorleif spoke then forty phrases and is this stave in:	Thorleif spoke forty verses and among them is this stave:
Oft með ærnri giftu öðlings himins röðla Jóta gramr hinn ítri Englandi roðið branda.	Often with merry luck noble heaven's wheel Jutland warrior the high-born England reddened swords.	Often with merry luck from noble heaven's wheel the high-born Jutland warrior reddened swords in England.
Konungur lofaði mjög kvæðið og allir þeir er heyrðu og sögðu bæði vel kveðið og skörulega fram flutt.	The-king praised much the-poem and all they who heard and said both well spoken and boldly forward performed.	The king praised the poem very much, and all those who heard it said it was both well spoken and boldly performed.

The Tale of Thorlief the Earl's Poet (Old Icelandic)

Old Icelandic	Literal	English
Konungur gaf Þorleifi að kvæðislaunum hring þann er stóð mörk og það sverð er til kom hálf mörk gulls og bað hann lengi með sér vera.	The-king gave Thorleif to poem's-reward a-ring then was stood a-mark and with a-sword was to come half a-mark of-gold and invited him long with him to-be.	The king gave Thorleif a reward for the poem, a ring that was worth a mark of gold, and a sword worth half a mark of gold, and he invited him to stay with him.
Þorleifur gekk til sætis og þakkaði vel konungi.	Thorleif went to sit and thanked well the-king.	Thorleif took his place and thanked the king well.
Og leið svo fram nokkura hríð og ekki lengi áður en Þorleifur ógladdist svo mjög að hann gáði varla undir drykkjuborð að ganga eða samsætis við sína bekkjunauta.	And passed so from some awhile and not long before that Thorleif un-gladdened so much that he cared scarcely up-to drinking-tables and went either banquet with himself bench-fellows.	And so it passed, and it was not long before Thorleif became so unhappy that he scarcely cared to go to the drinking tables to feast or talk with his bench mates.
Finnur konungur þetta bráðlega og lætur kalla Þorleif fyrir sig og mælti:	Found the-king this quickly and had called Thorleif before him and spoke:	The king soon noticed this and had Thorleif called before him, and asked:
"Hvað veldur ógleði þinni er þú gáir varla að halda háttum við oss?"	"What brought-about un-gladness yours that you care scarcely to hold custom with us?"	"What has brought about your unhappiness, that you hardly keep to our customs?"
Þorleifur svarar:	Thorleif answered:	Thorleif answered:
"Það munuð þér heyrt hafa herra að sá er skyldur að leysa annars vandræði er að spyr".	"That should you heard have lord that so who should to solve another's difficulty who that asks".	"You must have heard, lord, that he who asks another's difficulty should solve it for him".
"Segðu fyrst",	"Say-you first",	"Tell it first",
segir konungur.	said the-king.	said the king.
Þorleifur svarar:	Thorleif answered:	Thorleif answered:
"Eg hefi kveðið vísur nokkurar í vetur er eg kalla Konurvísur er eg hefi ort um Hákon jarl því að jarl er kona kenndur í skáldskap.	"If have poem verses some in winter that i call Woman-Verses that i have worded about Hakon earl because that the-earl is a-woman known in poetry.	"I have composed some verses in the winter, that I call Women Verses, that I composed about Earl Hakon, because the earl is called a woman in poetry.

The Tale of Thorlief the Earl's Poet (Old Icelandic)

Old Icelandic	Literal	English
Nú ógleður mig það herra ef eg fæ eigi orlof af yður að fara til Noregs og færa jarli kvæðið".	Now un-glad me that lord if i get not leave of yours to travel to Norway and bring the-earl the-poem".	I will be unhappy, lord, if I do not get your leave to travel to Norway to bring the earl the poem".
"Þú skalt að vísu fá orlof",	"You shall this certainly get leave",	"You shall certainly have leave",
segir konungur, "og skaltu þó heita oss áður að koma aftur til vor það fljótasta sem þú getur því að vér viljum þín ekki missa sakir íþrótta þinna".	said the-king, "and shall-you though promise us return to come after to spring the soonest as you get therefore that we wish your not miss sake skills yours".	said the king, "and you shall promise to return to us soon after spring, because we do not wish to miss your skills".
Þorleifur hét því og fékk sér nú farning og fór norður í Noreg og linnir eigi fyrr en hann kemur í Þrándheim.	Thorleif promised accordingly and got himself now passage and travelled north to Norway and stopped not before that he came to Trondheim.	Thorleif promised accordingly and now got himself passage to travel north to Norway, and did not stop until he came to Trondheim.
Þá sat Hákon jarl á Hlöðum.	Then sat Hakon earl at Lade.	Then Hakon sat in residence at Lade.
Þorleifur býr sér nú stafkarls gervi og bindur sér geitarskegg og tók sér eina stóra hít og lét koma undir stafkarls gervina og bjó svo um að öllum skyldi sýnast sem hann æti þann kost er hann kastaði í hítina því að gíman hennar var uppi við munn honum undir geitarskegginu.	Thorleif prepared himself now as-a-beggar character and bound himself goat-beard and took himself a large bag and had come-with under beggar's disguise and prepared so about that all should appear as he had then food that he cast in the-bag because that opening its was up by mouth his under goat-beard.	Thorleif now disguised himself as a beggar and wore a goat's beard, he also took a large bag which he kept under the disguise, and it was prepared so that everyone would think that he ate the food that he put into the bag, because the opening was up by his mouth under the goat's beard.
Síðan tekur hann hækjur tvær og var broddur niður úr hvorri, fer nú þar til er hann kemur á Hlaðir.	Afterwards took he crutches two and were spikes down out-of each, travelled now there until that he came to Lade.	Afterwards he also took two crutches with spikes on the ends, and travelled until he came to Lade.
Það var aðfangskveld jóla í þann tíma er jarl var kominn í sæti og mart stórmenni er jarl hafði að sér boðið til jólaveislunnar.	It was midwinter-evening Yule at that time when the-earl was coming to sit and many great-men that the-earl had that he invited to yule-feast.	It was the midwinter evening of Yule, when the earl was coming to sit, and there were many great men that the earl had invited to the Yule feast.

The Tale of Thorlief the Earl's Poet (Old Icelandic)

Old Icelandic	Literal	English
Karl gengur greiðlega inn í höllina en er hann kemur inn stumrar hann geysimjög og fellur fast á hækjurnar og snýr til annarra stafkarla og sest niður utarlega í hálminn.	The-old-man went quickly in to the-hall and when he came in stumbled he exceedingly-much and fell close had the-crutches and turned to other beggars and sat down out-lying of the-straw.	The old man went quickly into the hall, and when he came in, he stumbled and fell heavily on his crutches, then turned to the other beggars and sat down at the edge of the straw.
Hann var nokkuð bæginn við stafkarla og heldur harðleikinn en þeir þoldu illa er hann lét ganga á þeim stafina.	He was somewhat troubled with beggars and rather rough and they endured badly that he let go to them sticks.	He was irritable with the beggars and quite rough, and they were not happy with being knocked by his sticks.
Hrukku þeir undan og varð af þessu hark og háreysti svo að heyrði um alla höllina.	Drew they back and became of this noise and commotion so that heard about all the-hall.	They drew back and this caused noise and commotion so that all who were in the hall heard.
En er jarl verður þessa var spyr hann hvað valdi óhljóði þessu.	Then when the-earl became this was asked he what controlled unsoundly this.	Then when the earl was aware of this, he asked what caused this din.
Honum er sagt að stafkarl einn sé sá þar kominn að svo sé illur og úrigur að ekki láti ógert.	He was said that beggar one himself saw there coming that so being bad and unruly that not had undone.	He was told that a beggar had been seen who was so bad and unruly that he stopped at nothing.
Jarl bað kalla hann fyrir sig og svo var og gert.	Earl asked call-to him before him him and so was and done.	The earl asked him to be called before him, and so it was done.
En er karl kom fyrir jarl hafði hann mjög stutt um kvaðningar.	And when the-old-man came before the-earl had he much short about greeting.	And when the old man came before the earl, he greeted him shortly.
Jarl spurði hann að nafni, ætt og óðali.	Earl asked him of name, ancestry and estate.	The earl asked him his name, his ancestry, and his estate.
"Óvant er nafn mitt herra að eg heiti Níðungur Gjallandason og kynjaður úr Syrgisdölum af Svíþjóð hinni köldu.	"Not-lacking is name mine lord that i named Nidung Son-of-gjallandi and descended from Syrgsdalir in Sweden the cold.	"Not lacking is my name, lord, for I am named Nidung son of Gjallandi and descended from Syrgsdalir in Sweden the cold.
Er eg kallaður Níðungur hinn nákvæmi.	Am i called Nidung the pernickety.	I am called Nidung the pernickety.
Hefi eg víða farið og marga höfðingja heim sótt.	Have i widely travelled and many chieftains' homes sought.	I have travelled widely and sought many chieftains' homes.

The Tale of Thorlief the Earl's Poet (Old Icelandic)

Old Icelandic	Literal	English
Gerist eg nú gamall mjög svo að trautt má eg aldur minn segja sakir elli og óminnis.	Becoming i now old much so that scarcely may i age mine say with-conviction age of amnesia.	I am now becoming so old that scarcely may I say my age with conviction because of amnesia.
Hefi eg mikla spurn af höfðingskap yðrum og harðfengi, visku og vinsældum, lagasetning og lítillæti, örleik og allri atgervi".	Have i much learned of lordship yours and toughness, wisdom and popularity, legislation and humility, generosity and all deeds".	I have learned much of your lordship and toughness, wisdom and popularity, legislation and humility, and your generosity in all deeds".
"Hví ertu svo harðúðigur og illur viðskiptis frá því sem aðrir stafkarlar?"	"Why are-you so harsher and ill behaved from therefore as other beggars?"	"Why are you so much harsher and badly behaved than the other beggars?'"
Hann svarar:	He answered:	He answered:
"Hvað er örvænt um þann sem alls gengur andvana nema víls og vesaldar og ekki hefir það er þarf og lengi legið úti á mörkum og skógum þó að sá verði æfur við ellina og allt saman en vanur áður sæmd og sællífi af hinum dýrstum höfðingjum en vera nú hataður af hverjum þorpara lítils verðum".	"What is desperation about than as all going destitution taken advantage and wretchedness and not having that which needed and long laying out in marshes and forests though that so become angry with age and all together that experienced before honour and blessed-life of other dearest chieftains but becoming now hated of each peasant little worth".	"What is desperation about other than always going in destitution, taken advantage of by wretchedness, not having what is needed, laying for a long time in the marshes and forests, though becoming so angry with age, when altogether before having experienced a blessed life of the dearest chieftains, but becoming now hated by every peasant of little worth".
Jarl mælti:	The-earl spoke:	The earl spoke:
"Ertu nokkur íþróttamaður karl er þú segist þó með höfðingjum verið hafa?"	"Are-you anything excellent-man old-man that you say though with chieftains became have?"	"Are you excellent at anything, old man, as you say you have been with chieftains?"
Karl svarar það megi vera þó að nokkuð hafi til þess haft verið	The-old-man answered that may be though that somewhat have until this have been	The old man answered that it may be something like that:
"þá er eg var á ungum aldri.	"then when i was of young age.	"then when I was young in age.
Komi að því sem mælt er, að hverjum karli kemur að örverpi.	Comes to therefore as said is, to each man comes to decrepitude.	But it comes, as they say, decrepitude to each and every man.

The Tale of Thorlief the Earl's Poet (Old Icelandic)

Old Icelandic	Literal	English
Er það og talað að seigt er svöngum að skruma.	Is that also told that tough from hunger to swagger.	It is also said that it is difficult to swagger when hungry.
Mun eg og ekki við yður skruma herra nema þér látið gefa mér að eta því að svo dregur að mér af elli, svengd og þorsta að víst eigi fæ eg staðið uppi lengur.	Should i also not with you show-off lord unless you let give me to eat because that so drawn that i-am of age, hungry and thirsty and know not can i stand up for-long.	I can't show off to you, lord, unless you give me something to eat, because I am so drawn and with age, hungry and thirsty, and I do not know how long I can stand up for.
Er slíkt harðla óhöfðinglegt að spyrja ókunna menn í hvern heim en hugsa eigi hvað mönnum hentar því að allir eru með því eðli skapaðir að bæði þurfa át og drykkju".	It-is such hardly chieftain-like to ask unknown people into one's home but think not what peoples' requirements because that all are with therefore nature shaped that both need eat and drink".	It us hardly chieftain-like to ask strangers into one's home but not think about his requirements, because we are all shaped by nature to need both food and drink".
Jarl skipaði að honum skyldi gefa kost sæmilega sem honum þarfaði.	The-earl arranged that he should give food properly as he needed.	The earl arranged that he should be given food properly as he needed.
Var og svo gert.	Was also so done.	This was done.
En er karl kom undir borð tekur hann greiðlega til matar og ryður diska þá alla er næstir honum voru og hann náði til svo að þjónustumenn urðu að sækja kost í annan tíma.	Then the old-man came up-to the-tables took he promptly to food and cleared plates then all that nearest him were and he caught to so the servants became to sake provide for a-second time.	Then the old man came up to the tables, and he promptly took the food and cleared all the plates that were nearest to him, forcing the servants to provide a second helping.
Tók karl nú öngu ófreklegar til matar en fyrr.	Took the-old-man now not un-eagerly to food then before.	The old man was not just as eager as before.
Sýndist öllum sem hann æti en hann kastaði reyndar í hítina þá er fyrr var getið.	Seemed-to all that he ate but he cast actually in the-bag then as before was told-of.	It seemed to everyone that he ate, but the food was actually in the bag, as was told before.
Hlógu menn nú fast að karli þessum.	Laughed people now closely at the-old-man this.	People focused on the old man, and laughed.
Þjónustumenn töluðu að bæði væri að hann væri mikill og miðdigur enda gæti hann mikið etið.	Servants told that both were that he was great and broad-waist and got he much to-eat.	The servants said that he was both tall, and with a broad waist, and he could eat a lot.
Karl gaf sér ekki að því og gerði sem áður.	The-old-man gave himself not that then and did as before.	The old man did not react, and did as before.

The Tale of Thorlief the Earl's Poet (Old Icelandic)

Old Icelandic	Literal	English
# 5	# 5	# 5
En er ofan voru drykkjuborð gekk Níðungur karl fyrir jarl og mælti:	When that over were drinking-tables went Nidung the-old-man before the-earl and spoke:	When the drinking tables were removed, the old man Nidung went to the earl and spoke:
"Hafið þér nú þökk fyrir herra en þó eigið þér illa þjónustumenn er allt gera verr en þér segið fyrir.	"Have you now thanks for lord but though own you bad servants that all done worst than you said before.	"You have now my thanks, lord, but you have bad servants that did everything worse than you ordered.
En nú vildi eg að þér sýnduð mér lítillæti herra og hlýdduð kvæði því er eg hefi ort um yður".	But now wish i that to-you give-performance me a-little lord and listen-to poem because that i have worded about you".	But now I wish to give you a performance of my poem that I have composed about you".
Jarl mælti:	The-earl spoke:	The earl spoke:
"Hefir þú nokkuð fyrr kvæði ort um höfðingja?"	"Have you any before poems worded about chieftains?"	"Have you composed any poems about chieftains before?"
"Satt er það herra",	"True is that lord",	"That is true, lord",
kvað hann.	said he.	he said.
Jarl mælti:	The-earl spoke:	The earl spoke:
"Búið þar komi að gömlum orðskvið, að það er oft gott er gamlir kveða, og flyttu fram kvæðið karl en vér munum til hlýða".	"Done there comes that old proverb, that it is often good what old-man recites, and move forward poem old-man and we shall to listen".	"Done there is the proverb, that it is often good what an old man recites, so come forward with the poem, old man, and we shall listen".
Þá hefur karl upp kvæðið og kveður framan til miðs og þykir jarli lof í hverri vísu og finnur að þar er getið og í framaverka Eiríks sonar hans.	Then had the-old-man upped the-poem and said in-front-of the middle and thought the-earl praise in each verse and found that there was told-of and in previous-deeds Erik's son his.	Then the old man began the poem and recited it to the middle, and the earl thought that he heard praise in each verse, and found that there were tales told about his son Erik.

The Tale of Thorlief the Earl's Poet (Old Icelandic)

Old Icelandic	Literal	English
En er á leið kvæðið þá bregður jarli nokkuð undarlega við að óværi og kláði hleypur svo mikill um allan búkinn á honum og einna mest um þjóin að hann mátti hvergi kyrr þola og svo mikil býsn fylgdi þessum óværa að hann lét hrífa sér með kömbum þar sem þeim kom að.	But as it passed the-poem then tricked the-earl something strange from a restlessness and itching ran so much about all body of him and only most about thighs that he may each sit-still endure and so much strangeness followed this restlessness that he had scratched himself with combs there as they came to.	But as the poem continued, the earl was tricked into feeling a strange restlessness and an itching that ran all over his body, especially around his thighs so that he could hardly sit still, this uneasiness was so strange that he had scratched himself with combs wherever he could.
En þar sem þeim kom eigi að lét hann taka strigadúk og ríða á þrjá knúta og draga tvo menn milli þjóanna á sér.	Then there as they could not that had he taken sack-cloth and rose in three knots and drew two men between thighs for him.	Where he could not reach, he took a sack cloth and made three knots in it, and two men dragged it between his thighs for him.
Nú tók jarli illa að geðjast kvæðið og mælti:	Now took the-earl ill that liking the-poem and spoke:	Now the earl took badly to the poem and spoke:
"Kann þinn heljarkarl ekki betur að kveða því að mér þykir þetta eigi síður heita mega níð en lof og lát þú um batna ella tekur þú gjöld fyrir".	"Can you hellish-old-man not better to say because that to-me seems this not less call may abuse than praise and let you about better or take you repayment for".	"Can you not recite something better you hellish old man, because it seems to me more like abuse than praise, and make it better or you will be repaid for it".
Karl hét góðu um og hóf þá upp vísur og heita Þokuvísur og standa í miðju Jarlsníði og er þetta upphaf að:	The-old-man promised improvement about and began then up verses and named Fog-verses and stood in middle-of The-earl's-abuse and was this beginning this:	The old man promised improvement and then began verses named Fog Verses, which are in the middle of the Earl's Abuse, and the beginning was this:
Þoku dregr upp hið ytra, él festist hið vestra, mökkr mun náms, af nökkvi, naðrbings kominn hingað.	Fog draws up then outside, blizzard grips the west, thick-clouds shall take, of the-ship, dragon comes here.	Fog draws up then outside, a blizzard grips the west, thick clouds shall take, of the ship, the dragon comes here.
En er hann hafði úti Þokuvísur þá var myrkt í höllinni.	When that he had finished Fog-verses then was dark in the-hall.	When he had finished the Fog Verses, it was dark in the hall.
Og er myrkt er orðið í höllinni tekur hann aftur til Jarlsníðs.	And was dark was become in the-hall took he returning to Earl's-abuse.	And when it became dark in the hall, he began the Earl Abuse verses again.

The Tale of Thorlief the Earl's Poet (Old Icelandic)

Old Icelandic	Literal	English
Og er hann kvað hinn efsta og síðasta þriðjung þá var hvert járn á gangi það er í var höllinni án manna völdum og varð það margra manna bani.	And as he spoke the upper and last third then was each iron-weapon from moved it that in was the-hall without man's doing and became that many people dead.	And has he recited the third and last part, then each iron weapon that as in the hall moved without man's doing, and many men became dead.
Jarl féll þá í óvit en karl hvarf þá í brott að luktum dyrum og óloknum lásum.	The-earl fell then into unconsciousness but the-old-man disappeared then to away that shut doors and undone locks.	The earl then fell into unconsciousness, but the old man disappeared away through shut doors and undone locks.
En eftir afliðið kvæðið minnkaði myrkrið og gerði bjart í höllinni.	Then after following the-poem decreased the-darkness and it-was bright in the-hall.	Then following after the poem the darkness decreased, and it was bright again in the hall.
Jarl raknaði við og fann að honum hafði nær gengið níðið.	The-earl recovered from and found that to-him had near gone the-abuse.	The earl recovered and found that the abuse had come quite close to him.
Sá þá og vegsummerki að af var rotnað skegg allt af jarli og hárið öðrum megin reikar og kom aldrei upp síðan.	Saw then also evidence that off was decayed beard all of the-earl and hair other side parting and came never up since.	He also saw evidence of this, because his beard had decayed, along with the hair on one side of his parting, and it never came back.
Nú lætur jarl ræsta höllina og eru hinu dauðu út bornir.	Now had the-earl cleared the-hall and they-were the dead out carried.	Now the earl had the hall cleared and the dead were carried out.
Þykist hann nú vita að þetta mun Þorleifur verið hafa en karl engi annar og mun launað þykjast hafa honum mannalát og fjártjón.	Thought he now knew that this must Thorleif been had the old-man none other and should repay considered had he manslaughter and financial-loss.	He thought that he knew that the old man must have been none other than Thorleif, and that this was repayment for the manslaughter and his financial loss.
Liggur jarl nú í þessum meinlætum allan þennan vetur og mikið af sumrinu.	Laid the-earl now from this malignance all the winter and most of the-summer.	This malignance laid the earl low for all of the winter and most of the summer.

6

Það er af Þorleifi að segja að hann snýst til ferðar suður til Danmerkur og hefir það til leiðarnests sér sem hann ginnti af þeim í höllinni.	It was of Thorleif to say that he turned to travel south to Denmark and had it to food his as he tricked from them in the-hall.	As for Thorleif, he set to travel south to Denmark, and for his provisions he had the food that he had tricked from them in the hall.

The Tale of Thorlief the Earl's Poet (Old Icelandic)

Old Icelandic	Literal	English
En hversu lengi sem hann hefir á leið verið þá létti hann eigi sinni ferð fyrr en hann kom á fund Sveins konungs og tók hann við honum fegins hendi og spurði hann að ferðum sínum en Þorleifur sagði allt sem farið hafði.	Then however long as he had to journey made then relief he not his travel before that he came to find Svein the-king and received he with him relieved hands and asked he of journey his and Thorleif said all which gone had.	Then however long the journey was to be made, he had no relief in his travel until he came to find king Svein, and he received him well with relieved hands, and asked him of his journey, and Thorleif said how all had gone.
Konungur svarar:	The-king answered:	The king answered:
"Nú mun eg lengja nafn þitt og kalla þig Þorleif jarlaskáld".	"Now should i lengthen name yours and call you Thorleif Earl's-Poet".	"Now I should lengthen your name and call you Thorleif the Earl's Poet".
Þá kvað konungur vísu:	Then said the-king verse:	Then the king said a verse:
Grenndi Þorleifr Þrænda þengils hróðr fyr drengjum, *hafa ólítið ýtar jarls níð borið víða.* *Njörðr réð vestan virðum vellstæri brag færa brot lands galt gæti grálega leóns báru.*	Slendered Thorleif The-Tronds' the-prince renown before the-fellows, had no-little out the-earl's abuse carried widely. Njord ruled west worthiness well-sized poetry brought away lands repaid got malice the-lion's carried.	Thorleif slendered the Tronds the prince's renown before the fellows, had no-little out the earl's abuse carried widely. Njord ruled the western worth well-sized poetry brought away lands repaid got for the lion's malice carried.
Þorleifur sagði konungi að hann fýstist út til Íslands og beiddi konung orlofs að fara þegar að vori.	Thorleif told the-king that he desired out-from to Iceland and asked the-king vacations to travel there in the-spring.	Thorleif told the king that he wished to travel out to Iceland and asked the king leave to travel there in the spring.
En konungur sagði svo vera skyldu "vil eg gefa þér skip í nafnfesti með mönnum og reiða og þvílíkri áhöfn sem þér þarfast".	Then the-king said so be-it should "wish i to-give you a-ship in name-giving with people and transport and accordingly-like crew as you need".	The king said that it would be so, "I wish to give you a ship as a name-gift, with people and transport and crew as you need".
Nú er Þorleifur þar um veturinn í góðu yfirlæti en að vordögum býr hann skip sitt og lét í haf og byrjaði vel og kom skipi sínu við Ísland í á þá er Þjórsá heitir.	Now was Thorleif there about winter in good favour and of spring-days prepared he ship his and had to sea and began well and came ship his to Iceland in river then was Thjorsa named.	Thorleif was there for the winter in great favour, and at the beginning of spring he prepared his ship and put to sea, and began well and his ship came to Iceland, into the river that was named Thjorsa.

The Tale of Thorlief the Earl's Poet (Old Icelandic)

Old Icelandic	Literal	English
Það segja menn að Þorleifur kvæntist um haustið og fengi þeirrar konu er Auður hét og væri Þórðar dóttir er bjó í Skógum undir Eyjafjöllum, gilds bónda og stórauðigs, kominn af ætt Þrasa hins gamla.	It is-said people that Thorlief got-married about autumn and got there a-wife who Aud was-named and was Thord daughter that lived in Skogar under Eyjafjoll-Mountains, strong farmer and great-wealth, came of descendents Thrasi the old.	People say that Thorlief got married in the autumn and had a wife who was named Aud, and she was the daughter of Thord of Skogar under the Eyjafjoll mountains, who was a successful and wealthy farmer, descended from Thrasi the old.
Auður var kvenskörungur mikill.	Aud was noble-woman much.	Aud was very much a noble woman.
Þorleifur sat um veturinn í Skógum en um vorið eftir keypti hann land að Höfðabrekku í Mýdal og bjó þar síðan.	Thorleif sat about winter in Skogar but about spring afterwards bought he land at Hofdabrekka in Myrdal-Valley and settled there since.	Thorlief spent the winter in Skogar, but the following spring he bought land at Hofdabrekka in the Myrdal valley and settled thereafter.
7	7	7
En nú er þar til að taka er Hákon jarl er, að honum batnaði hins mesta meinlætis en það segja sumir menn að hann yrði aldrei samur maður og áður og vildi jarl nú gjarna hefna Þorleifi þessar smánar ef hann gæti, heitir nú á fulltrúa sína, Þorgerði Hörgabrúði og Irpu systur hennar, að reka þann galdur út til Íslands að Þorleifi ynni að fullu og færir þeim miklar fórnir og gekk til fréttar.	But now is there to from take that Hakon the-earl was, that he bettered his most malignancy but that said some people that he became never the-same man of before and wished the-earl now gladly avenge Thorleif this humiliation if he could, called now on delegates his, Thorgerd Horgabrudi and Irpu sister hers, to drive then sorcery out to Iceland to Thorleif win-over that full and carried them much sacrifices and got to omens.	Now to take to the Earl Hakon, he mostly recovered from this malignancy, but some people said that he was never the same man as before, and the earl now wished to gladly avenge Thorleif of this humiliation if he could, he called on his delegates, Thorgerd Horgabrudi and her sister Irpu, to drive sorcery out to Iceland to defeat Thorleif fully, and he carried them many offerings and got omens.

The Tale of Thorlief the Earl's Poet (Old Icelandic)

Old Icelandic	Literal	English
En er hann fékk þá frétt er honum líkaði lét hann taka einn rekabút og gera úr trémann og með fjölkynngi og atkvæðum jarls en tröllskap og fítonsanda þeirra systra lét hann drepa einn mann og taka úr hjartað og láta í þenna trémann og færðu síðan í föt og gáfu nafn og kölluðu Þorgarð og mögnuðu hann með svo miklum fjandans krafti að hann gekk og mælti við menn, komu honum síðan í skip og sendu hann út til Íslands þess erindis að drepa Þorleif jarlaskáld.	And when he got then omens that he liked had he taken a drift-wood and made of wooden-man and with witchcraft and songs earls and witchcraft and magic there sisters had he kill one man and taken out heart and had in this wooden-man and brought afterwards to clothing and gave name and called Thorgard and power he with so much devil's power that he walked and talked with people, came to-him afterwards to a-ship and sent him out to Iceland this errand to kill Thorleif Earl's-Poet.	And when he got the omens that he liked, he took some drift wood and made a wooden man, and with his witchcraft and songs, and with the magic of his sisters, he had a man killed to take his heart and place in the wooden man, and afterwards brought clothing and gave him a name and called him Thorgard, and with the strong power of the devil he walked and talked with people, he was put on a ship and sent to Iceland on an errand to kill Thorleif the Earl's poet.
Gyrti Hákon hann atgeir þeim er hann hafði tekið úr hofi þeirra systra og Hörgi hafði átt.	Equipped Hakon him a-halberd then that he had taken out-of temple theirs sisters and Horgi had belonged.	Hakon gave him a halberd that he had taken out of the temple that belonged to his sisters at Horgi.
Þorgarður kom út til Íslands í þann tíma er menn voru á alþingi.	Thorgard came out to Iceland in that time that men were in assembly.	Thorgard came to Iceland at the time when people were at the assembly.
Þorleifur jarlaskáld var á þingi.	Thorleif Earl's-Poet was at assembly.	Thorleif's the Earl's Poet was at the assembly.
Það var einn dag að Þorleifur gekk frá búð sinni er hann sá að maður gekk vestan yfir Öxará.	It was one day that Thorleif went from booth his when he saw that a-man walked from-the-west over Oxara.	One day Thorleif went from his booth and saw a man walking from the west over the Oxara river.
Sá var mikill vexti og illslegur í bragði.	Saw was large grown and evil-like in movement.	He saw that he was large and evil looking in his movement.
Þorleifur spyr þenna mann að heiti.	Thorleif asked this man of name.	Thorleif asked this man his name.
Hann nefndist Þorgarður og kastaði þegar kaldyrðum að Þorleifi en er Þorleifur heyrði það ætlaði hann að bregða sverðinu konungsnaut er hann var gyrður með en í þessu bili lagði Þorgarður atgeirnum á Þorleifi miðjum og í gegnum hann.	He was-named Thorgard and cast straightaway cold-bloodedly to Thorleif and when Thorleif heard this intended he to draw the-sword king's-gift that he was equipped-with with but in this moment laid Thorgard halberd to Thorleif's middle and in through him.	He said that his name was Thorgard and looked at him cold-bloodedly, and when Thorleif heard this, he intended to draw the sword that king Svein had given to him, but in that moment, Thorgard laid his halberd through his middle.

The Tale of Thorlief the Earl's Poet (Old Icelandic)

Old Icelandic	Literal	English
En er hann fékk lagið hjó hann til Þorgarðs en hann steyptist í jörðina niður svo að í iljarnar var að sjá.	Then when he got laid struck he to Thorgard then he disappeared into the-earth down so that for soles-of-the-feet was to see.	Then when he was hit, he struck at Thorgard, but he had disappeared down into the earth so that only the soles of his feet could be seen.
Þorleifur snaraði að sér kyrtilinn og kvað vísu:	Thorleif twisted about himself tunic and spoke verse:	Thorleif twisted his tunic about him and spoke a verse:
Hvarf hinn hildardjarfi, *hvað varð af Þorgarði?* *villumaðr á velli,* *vígdjarfr refilstiga.*	Disappeared the courageous-warrior, what became of Thorgard? villain in the-fields, slaying-warrior mysterious-path.	The courageous warrior disappeared, what became of Thorgard? the villain in the fields, the slaying warrior's mysterious path.
Farið hefir Gautr að grjóti *gunnelds hinn fjölkunni,* *síðan mun hann í helju* *hvílast stund og mílu.*	Gone has Odin to rocks battle-fire the skilled-in-magic, after shall he in Hel rest awhile and mile.	Odin has gone to the rocks, battle-fired the skills in magic, after shall be in Hel and rest awhile a mile.
Þá gekk Þorleifur heim til búðar sinnar og sagði mönnum þenna atburð og þótti öllum mikils um vert um þenna atburð.	Then went Thorleif home to booth his and told people these events and thought all much about had-been about these events.	Thorleif went back to his booth and told people of these events, and people thought much about these events.
Síðan varpar Þorleifur frá sér kyrtlinum og féllu þá út iðrin og lét Þorleifur þar líf sitt við góðan orðstír og þótti mönnum það allmikill skaði.	Afterwards threw Thorleif from himself tunic and fell then out bowels and laid Thorleif there life his with good fame and thought people that all-great harm.	Afterwards Thorleif threw off his tunic and his bowels spilled out, and he laid his life there with good fame, and all people thought that this was a great harm.
Þóttust nú allir vita að Þorgarður þessi hafði engi verið annar en galdur og fjölkynngi Hákonar jarls.	Thought now all certainly that Thorgard this had none been other than sorcery and witchcraft Hakon's the-earl.	They thought that it was certain that this Thorgard had been none other than the sorcery and witchcraft of Earl Hakon.
Síðan var Þorleifur heygður.	Afterwards was Thorleif buried.	Afterwards Thorleif was buried.
Haugur hans stendur norður af lögréttu og sést hann enn.	Mound his stood north of law-assembly and seen he was.	His mound stood north of the law assembly and could be seen from there.

The Tale of Thorlief the Earl's Poet (Old Icelandic)

Old Icelandic	Literal	English
Bræður hans voru á þingi er þetta var tíðinda og gerðu útferð Þorleifs sæmilega og erfðu hann að fornum sið en Ásgeir faðir þeirra var þá litlu andaður.	Brothers his was at assembly when this was news and made funeral Thorleif's fair and inherited he the ancient traditions as Asgeir father theirs was then recently died.	His brothers were at the assembly when this became news, and they gave Thorleif a fair funeral feast according to the ancient traditions that his father Asgeir had when he recently died.
Síðan fóru menn heim af þingi og fréttust þessi tíðindi nú víða um Ísland og þóttu mikils verð.	Afterwards went people home from assembly and reported this news now widely about Iceland and thought a-great price.	Afterwards people went home from the assembly and reported this news widely about Iceland, and everyone thought it a great cost.

8

Old Icelandic	Literal	English
Sá maður bjó þá á Þingvelli er Þorkell hét.	So a-man lived then at Thingvellir who-was Thorkell named.	So there was a man who lived that Thingvellir and was named Thorkell.
Hann var auðigur maður að ganganda fé og hafði jafnan hægt í búi.	He was wealthy man as went cattle and had equally comfortable in farm.	He was a wealth man with regard to cattle, and had a comfortable farm.
Engi var hann virðingamaður.	None was he man-of-high-rank.	He was not a man of high rank.
Sauðamaður hans hét Hallbjörn og var kallaður hali.	Shepherd his named Hallbjorn and was called Hali.	He shepherd was named Hallbjorn but people called him Hali (Tail).
Hann vandist oftlega til að koma á haug Þorleifs og svaf þar um nætur og hélt þar nálægt fé sínu.	He did often to that came to mound Thorleif's and slept there about night and held there close cattle his.	He often came to Thorleif's mound and slept there through the night and held his cattle close there.
Kemur honum það jafnan í hug að hann vildi geta ort lof kvæði nokkurt um haugbúann og talar það jafnan er hann liggur á hauginum en sakir þess að hann var ekki skáld og hann hafði þeirrar listar eigi fengið fékk hann ekki kveðið og komst aldrei lengra áfram fyrir honum um skáldskapinn en hann byrjaði svo:	Came he that equally in thoughts that he wished get words praise poem some about the-mound-dweller and said that usually when he lay about the-mound but for-the-sake this that he was not poet and he had there art not got went he not poem but came never longer not-further for him about poetry that he began so:	Thoughts often came to him that he wished to compose words of praise about the mound dweller, and he usually said so when he lay about the mound, but because he was not a good poet and did not have the gift, he never managed to compose anything longer than the beginning:
Hér liggr skáld.	Here lies a-poet.	Here lies a poet.

The Tale of Thorlief the Earl's Poet (Old Icelandic)

Old Icelandic	Literal	English
En meira gat hann ekki kveðið.	Then more could he not put-to-words.	Then he could not put more to words.
Það var eina nátt sem oftar að hann liggur á hauginum og hefir hina sömu iðn fyrir stafni ef hann gæti aukið nokkuð lof um haugbúann.	It was one night as often that he laid about the-mound and had then same craft for staves if he got increase some praise about the-mound-dweller.	One night as usual he was lying on the mound and was still trying to craft some verses and write any more n praise about the mound dweller.
Síðan sofnar hann og eftir það sér hann að opnast haugurinn og gengur þar út maður mikill vexti og vel búinn.	Afterwards slept he and after that saw he that open the-mound and went there out a-man great grown and well prepared.	Then he fell asleep and after that he saw that the mound opened, and a large man came out, and he was well dressed.
Hann gekk upp á hauginn að Hallbirni og mælti:	He went up to the-mound to Hallbjorn and spoke:	He went up to the mound and said to Hallbjorn:
"Þar liggur Hallbjörn og vildir þú fást í því sem þér er ekki lánað, að yrkja lof um mig og er það annaðhvort að þér verður lagið í þessi íþrótt og munt þú það af mér fá meira en vel flestum mönnum öðrum og er það vænna að svo verði ella þarftu ekki í þessu að brjótast lengur.	"There lies Hallbjorn and wish you get with therefore which you are not gifted, that compose praise about me and is that either-way that you become have of this skilled and shall you that of me have more than well most people others and is that good that so becomes or need not of this to break longer.	"There you lie, Hallbjorn, and you would like to catch something not in your power, to compose praise about me, and either you will become skilled and you can get this from me more than others, as is likely to happen, or else there is no need for you to continue any longer.
Skal eg nú kveða fyrir þér vísu og ef þú getur numið vísuna og kannt hana þá er þú vaknar þá munt þú verða þjóðskáld og yrkja lof um marga höfðingja og mun þér í þessi íþrótt mikið lagið verða".	Shall i now speak before you verse and if you can take verse and know it then when you awake then shall you become skilled-poet and compose praise about many chieftains and should you in this skilled much have become".	I shall now speak a verse for you, and if you can take this verse and know it, then when you awake, you shall become a skilled poet and compose praise about many chieftains, and you shall have become much skilled in this".
Síðan togar hann á honum tunguna og kvað vísu þessa:	Afterwards pulled he of his tongue and spoke verse this:	Then he pulled his tongue and spoke this verse:
Hér liggr skáld það er skálda	Here lies poet that is of-poets	Here lies a poet that is of all poets
var mestr að flestu.	was the-greatest of. the-most	he was the greatest of the most.
Naddveiti frá eg nýtan	Provided-knowing from i am-able	I hear that he was able
níð Hákoni smíða.	abuse of-Hakon created.	to craft abuse of Hakon.
Áðr gat engr né síðan	After got none nor afterwards	None before or after,

The Tale of Thorlief the Earl's Poet (Old Icelandic)

Old Icelandic	Literal	English
annarra svo manna, frægt hefir orðið það fyrðum, férán lokið hánum.	others so people, fame had words that warriors, plunder end his.	of so many other people, had fame of words that warriors ended his plunder.
"Nú skaltu svo hefja skáldskapinn að þú skalt yrkja lofkvæði um mig þá er þú vaknar og vanda sem mest bæði hátt og orðfæri og einna mest kenningar".	"Now shall so begin poetry that you shall compose praise-words about me then when you awake and care that most both high and vocabulary and only the-best kennings".	"Now you shall begin your poetry that you shall compose words of praise about me, then when you awake, take care that it is both high in vocabulary and the best kennings".
Síðan hverfur hann aftur í hauginn og lýkst hann aftur en Hallbjörn vaknar og þykist sjá á herðar honum.	Afterwards turned he back into the-mound and closed he returned then Hallbjorn awoke and thought saw of shoulders his.	Afterwards he turned back into the mound and it closed behind him, then Hallbjorn awoke and thought he saw his shoulders.
Síðan kunni hann vísuna og fór síðan til byggða heim með fé sitt eftir tíma og sagði þenna atburð.	Afterwards knew he verse and travelled since to settlement home with wealth his after time and said then events.	Afterwards he remembered the verse and then went back to the farm with his flock after a time and told of these events.
Orti Hallbjörn síðan lofkvæði um haugbúann og var hið mesta skáld og fór utan fljótlega og kvað kvæði um marga höfðingja og fékk af þeim miklar virðingar og góðar gjafir og græddi af því stórfé, og gengur af honum mikil saga bæði hér á landi og útlendis þó að hún sé hér eigi rituð.	Words Hallbjorn since praise-words about the-mound-dweller and was then the-best poet and travelled out soon and spoke poems about many chieftains and got of them much honour and good gifts and profit of therefore great-wealth, and went of him much stories both here about the-land and other-lands though that it being here not written.	Hallbjorn composed since words of praise about the mound dweller and was the best poet, and he frequently travelled abroad and composed poems about many chieftains and received from them much honour and good gifts from them, and his wealth increased, and there went many stories about him both in Iceland and abroad, but they are not written down here.
En frá bræðrum Þorleifs er það að segja að næsta sumar eftir andlát hans fóru þeir utan, Ólafur völubrjótur og Helgi hinn frækni, og ætluðu til hefnda eftir bróður sinn.	Then from brothers Thorleif's was it to say that next summer after death his travelled they out, Olaf knuckle-breaker and Helgi the brave, and supposed to revenge after brother theirs.	Then to Thorleif's brothers to say that the next summer after his death day, Olaf knuckle-breaker and Helgi the brave travelled out and intended to get revenge for their brother.
En þeim varð eigi lagið þá enn að standa yfir höfuðsvörðum Hákonar jarls því að hann hafði þá enn eigi öllu illu því fram farið sem honum varð lagið sér til skammar og skaða.	But they were not laid then but to stand over head-skin Hakon's the-earl because that he had then but not all evil such from going as he was laid to-him to shame and damage.	But they were not yet fated to have Earl Hakon's scalp, because he had not yet done all of the evil which was destined for his shame and harm.

The Tale of Thorlief the Earl's Poet (Old Icelandic)

Old Icelandic	Literal	English
En þó brenndu þeir mörg hof fyrir jarlinum og gerðu honum margan fjárskaða í ránum og hervirki er þeir veittu honum og margri annarri óspekt.	But though burned they many temples for the-earl and did to-him many wealth-damage in robbery and plundering that they granted him and many other disturbances.	But they managed to burn many of the earl's temples, and did much to damage his wealth with robbery and plundering, and they granted him many other disturbances.
Og lýkur hér frá Þorleifi að segja.	And ends here from Thorleif to say.	And this is the end of what there is to say about Thorleif.

Word List *(Old Icelandic to English)*

Old Icelandic	English
A, a	
að	a, about, and, as, at, for, from, in, it, of, that, the, then, this, to
aðfangskveld	midwinter-evening
aðrar	other
aðrir	other, others
af	from, from, in, of, of, off
afliðið	following
aftur	after, back, returned, returning
afturreka	back-driven
aldrei	never
aldri	age
aldur	age
alfari	for-good
alla	all, all
allan	all
allir	all
allmikill	all-great
allri	all
alls	all
allt	all, all
alþingi	assembly
andaður	died
andar	soul
andlát	death
andvana	destitution
annaðhvort	either-way
annan	a-second
annar	another, other
annarra	other, others
annarri	other
annars	another's
atburð	events
atburðir	events
atgeir	a-halberd
atgeirnum	halberd
atgervi	deeds
atgervimaður	accomplished-man
atkvæðum	songs
auðigur	wealthy
Auður	Aud (name), Aud (name)
aukið	increase
austur	east
Á, á	
á	about, at, for, from, had, in, it, of, on, river, that, this, to
áðr	after
áður	before, return
áfram	not-further
áhöfn	crew
án	without
ánauð	enslavement
Ásgeir	Asgeir (name)
Ásgeiri	Asgeir (name)
ásjá	assistance
ástfóstur	foster-care
ásum	poles
át	eat
átján	eighteen
átt	belonged, had
áttu	had
Æ, æ	
æfur	angry
ærnri	merry
æti	ate, had
ætlaði	intended
ætluðu	supposed
ætt	ancestors, ancestry, descendents
ævintýr	adventure
B, b	
bað	asked, bid, invited

Word List (Old Icelandic to English)

Old Icelandic	English
báðir	both
bæði	both
bæginn	troubled
bani	dead
báru	carried
batna	better
batnaði	bettered
báts	boats
beiddi	asked
beiddist	asked
bekkjunauta	bench-fellows
betur	better
biður	asked
bili	moment
binda	bound, tied-up
bindur	bound
bjart	bright
bjó	lived, prepared, settled
blekkir	deceived
Blönduósi	Blonduos (place)
blygðar	shame
boðið	invited
böggva	the-mauler
bölvaðra	cursed
bónda	farmer
borð	the-tables
borið	carried
bornir	carried
bráðlega	quickly
bræðrum	brothers
bræður	brothers
brag	poetry
bragði	movement
branda	swords
bregða	draw
bregður	tricked
Brekku	Brekka (place)
brenna	burned, burnt
brenndu	burned
brjótast	break
broddur	spikes
bróður	brother
brot	away
brott	away
búð	booth

Old Icelandic	English
búðanna	booths
búðar	booth
búi	farm
búið	done, settled
búinn	prepared
búkinn	body
burt	away
byggða	settlement
býr	prepared
byrjaði	began
byrjar	fair-wind
býsn	strangeness

D, d

Old Icelandic	English
dæmt	deem
dag	day
daginn	the-day
dálegra	harmful
Danmerkur	Denmark (place)
dauðu	dead
diska	plates
dögum	days
dökkri	dark
dóttir	daughter
draga	drew
drápu	phrases
dregr	draws
dregur	drawn
drekktur	drowned
drengjum	the-fellows
drengr	men
drepa	kill
drykkju	drink
drykkjuborð	drinking-tables
dýflissu	dungeon
dýrstum	dearest
dyrum	doors

E, e

Old Icelandic	English
eða	either, or
eðli	nature
ef	if

Word List (Old Icelandic to English)

Old Icelandic	English
efnilegir	promising
efsta	upper
eftir	after, afterwards
eftirmáls	after-the-case
eg	i, if
eiga	not
eigi	not
eigið	own
eign	owning
eina	a, one
einn	a, one
einna	only
Eiríks	Erik's (name)
ekki	not
ella	or
elli	age
ellina	age
elsti	eldest
en	and, as, but, than, that, the, then, when
enda	and, end
engi	none
Englandi	England (place)
engr	none
enn	but, was
er	am, are, as, from, has, is, it-is, that, the, was, what, when, which, who, who-was
erfðu	inherited
erindis	errand
ertu	are-you
eru	are, they-were, we-are
eta	eat
etið	to-eat
Eyjafjöllum	Eyjafjoll-Mountains (place)
eymd	misery
eyri	sand

É, é

Old Icelandic	English
él	blizzard

F, f

Old Icelandic	English
fá	get, have
faðir	father
fæ	can, get
færa	bring, brought
færðu	brought
færir	carried
Fagurkinn	Fair-Cheek (name)
fann	found
fara	travel
fararefna	travel-goods
farið	going, gone, travelled
farning	passage
fast	close, closed, closely
fást	get
fé	cattle, wealth
fegins	relieved
fékk	got, went
félaga	companions
féll	fell
féllu	fell
fellur	fell
fengi	got
fengið	caught, got
fer	travelled, went
férán	plunder
ferð	travel
ferðar	travel
ferðum	journey
fertuga	forty
festist	grips
fíl	elephant
finnur	found
fítonsanda	magic
fjandans	devil's
fjárhlut	fee-lot, financial-share
fjárskaða	wealth-damage
fjártjón	financial-loss
fjölkunni	skilled-in-magic
fjölkynngi	witchcraft
fjölmenni	following-men
fleira	more
flestu	the-most
flestum	most

Word List (Old Icelandic to English)

Old Icelandic	English
fljótasta	soonest
fljótlega	soon
flutt	performed
flytja	to-carry
flyttu	move
föður	father
fór	travelled, went
fornfræði	ancient-ways
fórnir	sacrifices
fornlegum	ancient-ways
fornum	ancient
forsmáður	shamed
fóru	travelled, went
förunauta	companions
fóstra	foster-father
fóstri	fostered
föt	clothing
frá	from
fræðum	instruction
frægt	fame
frækni	brave
frænda	kinsmen
fram	forward, from
framan	in-front-of
framaverka	previous-deeds
framleiðslu	causing
frásagnar	from-told
frétt	omens
fréttar	omens
fréttist	sought
fréttust	reported
fullkomið	full-coming
fulltingi	assistance
fulltrúa	delegates
fullu	full
fund	find, meet
fylgdi	followed
fylgt	followed
fyr	before
fyrðum	warriors
fyrir	before, before him, for
fyrr	before
fyrst	first
fýsi	desire
fýstist	desired

G, g

Old Icelandic	English
gáði	cared
gæti	could, got
gaf	gave
gáfu	gave
gáir	care
galdur	sorcery
galt	repaid
gamall	old
gamla	old
gamlir	old-man
ganga	go, went
ganganda	went
gangi	moved
Gáseyri	Gaseyri (place)
gat	could, got
Gautr	Odin (name)
geðjast	liking
gefa	give, to-give
gegnum	through
geitarskegg	goat-beard
geitarskegginu	goat-beard
gekk	got, walked, went
gengið	gone
gengur	going, went
ger	made
gera	done, made
gerði	did, had-done, it-was
gerðist	happened
gerðu	did, made
gerist	becoming
gerningum	witchcraft
gert	done
gervi	character
gervilegur	talented
gervina	disguise
geta	get
getið	told-of
getur	can, get
geysimjög	exceedingly-much
giftu	luck
gilds	strong
gildur	capable

Word List (Old Icelandic to English)

Old Icelandic	English	*Old Icelandic*	English
gíman	opening	*hákoni*	of-Hakon
ginnti	tricked	*halda*	hold
gjafir	gifts	*hálf*	half
gjalda	repay	*Hali*	Hali (name)
gjallandason	son-of-gjallandi	*Hallbirni*	Hallbjorn (name)
gjarna	gladly	*Hallbjörn*	Hallbjorn (name)
gjöld	repayment	*hálminn*	the-straw
glögglega	clearly	*hana*	it
goða	the-chieftain	*hann*	he, him
góða	food	*hans*	he, his
góðan	good	*hánum*	his
góðar	good	*harðfengi*	toughness
goði	chieftain	*harðla*	hardly
góðu	good, improvement	*harðleikinn*	rough
göldrum	magical-arts	*harðúðigur*	harsher
gömlum	old	*háreysti*	commotion
góss	belongings	*hárið*	hair
gott	good	*hark*	noise
græddi	profit	*háseta*	first-mate
grálega	malice	*hásetum*	crew
gramr	warrior	*hataður*	hated
greiðlega	promptly, quickly	*hátt*	high
grenndi	slendered	*háttum*	custom
grjóti	rocks	*haug*	mound
guðníðingskapur	idol-worship	*haugbúann*	the-mound-dweller
Guðs	God (name)	*hauginn*	the-mound
gulls	of-gold	*hauginum*	the-mound
gunnelds	battle-fire	*haugur*	mound
gyrður	equipped-with	*haugurinn*	the-mound
gyrti	equipped	*haustið*	autumn
		hefi	have
		hefir	had, has, have, having

H, h

		hefja	begin
hægt	comfortable, possible	*hefna*	avenge
hækjur	crutches	*hefnda*	revenge
hækjurnar	the-crutches	*hefur*	had
haf	sea	*hegningartíminn*	punishment-time
hafa	had, have	*heim*	home, homes
hafði	had	*heita*	call, named, promise
hafi	have	*heiti*	name, named
hafið	have	*heitir*	called, named
haft	have	*heldur*	rather
Hákon	Hakon (name)	*Helgi*	Helgi (name)
Hákonar	Hakon (name), Hakon's (name)	*heljarkarl*	hellish-old-man
		Helju	Hel (place)

Word List (Old Icelandic to English)

Old Icelandic	English
hélt	held
hendi	hands
hengja	hanged
hennar	hers, its
hentar	requirements
hentugri	more-convenient
hér	here
herðar	shoulders
herra	lord
hervirki	plundering
hét	named, promised, was-named
heygður	buried
heyrði	heard
heyrðu	heard
heyrið	hear
heyrt	heard
hið	the, then
hildardjarfi	courageous-warrior
himins	heaven's
hina	then
hingað	here
hinn	the, those
hinni	the
hins	his, the
hinu	the
hinum	other
hít	bag
hítina	the-bag
hitti	met
hjartað	heart
hjó	struck
Hlaðajarl	Earl-Of-Lade (name)
Hlaðajarls	Earl-Of-Lade (name)
Hlaðir	Lade (place)
hleypur	ran
Hlöðum	Lade (place)
hlógu	laughed
hlýða	listen, to-hear
hlýdduð	listen-to
hof	temples
hóf	began
Höfðabrekku	Hofdabrekka (place)
höfðingja	chieftains, chieftains'
höfðingjum	chieftains
höfðingskap	lordship

Old Icelandic	English
hofi	temple
höfuðsvörðum	head-skin
höfum	have
höllina	the-hall
höllinni	the-hall
honum	he, he-had, him, his, to-him
Hörgabrúði	Horgabrudi (name)
Hörgi	Horgi (place)
hríð	awhile
hrífa	scratched
hring	a-ring
hróðr	renown
hrollir	shivering
hrukku	drew
hug	thoughts
hugr	heart
hugsa	think
hún	it, she
hvað	what
hvarf	disappeared
hver	who
hverfur	turned
hvergi	each
hverjum	each, who's
hvern	one's
hverri	each
hversu	however, how-so
hvert	each
hví	why
hvílast	rest
hvorri	each
hvort	whether

I, i

Old Icelandic	English
ið́n	craft
iðrin	bowels
iljarnar	soles-of-the-feet
illa	bad, badly, ill
illslegur	evil-like
illu	evil
illur	bad, ill
inn	in
Irpu	Irpu (name)

Word List (Old Icelandic to English)

Old Icelandic	English

Í, í

Old Icelandic	English
í	about, at, for, from, in, into, of, to, with
Ísland	Iceland (place)
Íslandi	Iceland (place)
Íslands	Iceland (place)
íþrótt	skilled
íþrótta	skills
íþróttamaður	excellent-man
íþróttir	skilled
ítri	high-born

J, j

Old Icelandic	English
jafnan	equally, usually
jarl	earl, the-earl
Jarlaskáld	Earl's-Poet (name)
jarli	earl, the-earl
jarlinn	the-earl
jarlinum	the-earl
jarls	earls, the-earl, the-earl's
jarlsníði	the-earl's-abuse
jarlsníðs	earl's-abuse
járn	iron-weapon
Jóla	Yule (name)
jólaveislunnar	yule-feast
jörðina	the-earth
Jóta	Jutland (place)

K, k

Old Icelandic	English
kaldyrðum	cold-bloodedly
kalla	call, called, call-to
kallaður	called
kann	can
kannt	know
Karl	Karl (name), old-man, the-old-man
karli	man, the-old-man
kastaði	cast
kaupir	bought
kaupmönnum	trading-men
kaupslagar	bargaining
kaupstaðinn	market-town
kaupunauta	customers
kaupunautar	customers
kemur	came, comes
kenna	teach
kenndur	known
kenningar	kennings
keypti	bought
kláði	itching
Klaufa	Klaufi (name)
knarrar	merchant-ships, of-the-ship
knúta	knots
kol	the-coals
köld	cold
köldu	cold
köldum	cold
kölluðu	called
kolum	coals
kom	came, come, could
koma	came, come, come-with
komast	come
kömbum	combs
komi	comes
kominn	came, comes, coming
komst	came
komu	came
kona	a-woman, wife, woman
konu	a-wife
konung	the-king
konungi	the-king
konungs	the-king
konungsnaut	king's-gift
konungur	the-king
Konurvísur	Woman-Verses (name)
kost	food, provide
krafti	power
krókóttum	devious
kunni	knew
kvað	said, spoke
kvaddi	greeted

Word List (Old Icelandic to English)

Old Icelandic	English
kvaðningar	greeting
kvæði	poem, poems
kvæðið	poem, the-poem
kvæðislaunum	poem's-reward
kvæntist	got-married
kvala	torment
kveða	recites, say, speak
kveðið	poem, put-to-words, spoken
kveður	said
kveldið	evening
kvenskörungur	noble-woman
kyndugskap	cunning
kynferði	kinsmen-origins
kynjaður	descended
kynstrum	strange
kyrr	sit-still
kyrtilinn	tunic
kyrtlinum	tunic

L, l

lætur	had, left
lagasetning	legislation
lagði	had, laid
lagið	have, laid
lánað	gifted
land	land, the-land
landi	the-land
lands	lands
lásum	locks
lát	let
láta	allow, had
láti	had
látið	let
laun	secrecy
launað	repay
legið	laying
leið	journey, passed
leiðarnests	food
leitaði	sought
lengi	long
lengja	lengthen
lengra	longer
lengur	for-long, longer

Old Icelandic	English
leóns	the-lion's
lét	had, laid, let
létti	relief
leysa	solve
líf	life
lífsdaga	life-days
lífstíma	lifetime
liggr	lies
liggur	laid, lay, lies
líkaði	liked
líkama	body
líkar	like
linnir	stopped
listar	art
lítillæti	a-little, humility
lítils	little
lítinn	little
litlu	recently
Ljótólfi	Ljotolf (name)
Ljótólfs	Ljotolf (name)
Ljótólfur	Ljotolf (name)
ljótu	ghastly
lof	praise
lofaði	praised
lofkvæði	praise-words
lögréttu	law-assembly
lokið	end
luktum	shut
lýkst	closed
lýkur	ends

M, m

má	may
maður	a-man, man
mælt	said
mælti	spoke, talked
mál	matter
mann	man
manna	man's, men, men, people
mannalát	manslaughter
manni	people
mannillska	man-evil
manninn	people

Word List (Old Icelandic to English)

Old Icelandic	English
marga	many
margan	many
margir	many
margkunnandi	many-known
margra	many, much
margri	many
mart	many
matar	food
mátti	may
með	with
mega	may
megi	may
megin	side
meinlætis	malignancy
meinlætum	malignance
meir	more
meira	more
menn	men, people
mér	i-am, me, to-me
mest	most, the-best
mesta	most, the-best
mesti	most
mestr	the-greatest
miðdigur	broad-waist
Miðfirði	Midfjord (place)
Miðfjarðar-Skeggja	Midfjorder-Skeggi (name)
miðju	middle-of
miðjum	middle
miðs	middle
mig	me, shall-i
mikið	most, much
mikil	much
mikill	great, large, much
mikils	a-great, much
mikinn	much
mikla	much
miklar	much
miklum	much
milli	between
mílu	mile
minn	mine
minnkaði	decreased
mislíkaði	misliked
missa	miss
mitt	mine

Old Icelandic	English
mjög	much
móður	mother
móðurbróður	mother's-brother
mögnuðu	power
mökkr	thick-clouds
mönnum	men, people, peoples'
mörg	many
mörgum	many
morguninn	morning
mörk	a-mark
mörkum	marshes
mun	must, shall, should
mundi	would
mundu	would
munn	mouth
munt	shall
munuð	shall, should
munum	shall
Mýdal	Myrdal-Valley (place)
myrkrið	the-darkness
myrkt	dark

N, n

Old Icelandic	English
naddveiti	provided-knowing
náði	caught
naðrbings	dragon
nær	near
næsta	next
næstir	nearest
nætur	night
nafn	name
nafnfesti	name-giving
nafni	name
nákvæmi	pernickety
nálægt	close
nam	took
náms	take
nátt	night
náttúra	nature
né	nor
nefndist	was-named
nema	except, taken, unless
níð	abuse
níðið	the-abuse

Word List (Old Icelandic to English)

Old Icelandic	English
Níðungur	Nidung (name)
niður	down
nítján	nineteen
Njörðr	Njord (name)
nokkuð	any, some, something, somewhat
nokkur	anything
nokkura	some
nokkurar	some
nokkurt	some
nökkvi	the-ship
norður	north
Noreg	Norway (place)
Noregs	Norway (place)
nóttina	the-night
nú	now
numið	take
nýtan	am-able

O, o

Old Icelandic	English
ofan	over
ofanverðum	the-uppermost
ofléttlega	willingly
oft	often
oftar	often
oftlega	often
og	also, and, but, of
opnast	open
orð	words
orðfæri	vocabulary
orðið	become, words
orðskvið	proverb
orðstír	fame
orlof	leave
orlofs	vacations
ort	worded, words
orti	words
oss	us, we

Ó, ó

Old Icelandic	English
óbætilegs	un-redeemable
óðali	estate
ófreklegar	un-eagerly
ógert	undone
ógladdist	un-gladdened
ógleði	un-gladness
ógleður	un-glad
óhljóði	unsoundly
óhöfðinglegt	chieftain-like
ókunna	unknown
Ólafs	Olaf's (name)
Ólafur	Olaf (name)
ólítið	no-little
óloknum	undone
óminnis	amnesia
óspekt	disturbances
óværa	restlessness
óværi	restlessness
óvant	not-lacking
óvinarins	the-enemy's
óvit	unconsciousness

Ö, ö

Old Icelandic	English
öðlings	noble
öðrum	other, others
öldu	wave
öllu	all
öllum	all, of-all
önga	none
öngu	not
örleik	generosity
örvænt	desperation
örverpi	decrepitude
Öxará	Oxara (place)

P, p

Old Icelandic	English
peninga	money

R, r

Old Icelandic	English
ráðum	advice
ræður	hired
rændi	robbed

Word List (Old Icelandic to English)

Old Icelandic	English
ræsta	cleared
raknaði	recovered
ránum	robbery
Rauðfeldur	Red-Cloak (name)
Rauði	Red (name)
réð	ruled
refilstiga	mysterious-path
reiða	transport
reikar	parting
reka	drive
rekabút	drift-wood
Reykjum	Reykir (place)
reyndar	actually
ríða	rose
ríkur	powerful
rís	rose
rituð	written
roðið	reddened
röðla	wheel
rotnað	decayed
ryðja	cleared
ryður	cleared

S, s

Old Icelandic	English
sá	saw, so
sækja	sake
sællífi	blessed-life
sæmd	honour
sæmilega	fair, properly
sæti	sit
sætis	sit
saga	stories
sagði	said, said, told
sagður	said
sagt	said
sakir	for-the-sake, sake, with-conviction
saman	together
samsætis	banquet
samur	the-same
sannlega	truly
sat	sat
satt	true
sauðamaður	shepherd
sé	being, himself, see
segðu	say-you
segið	said
segir	said
segist	say
segja	is-said, said, say
seigt	tough
selja	to-sell
sem	as, that, what, which
sendu	sent
sér	for-himself, he, he-himself, him, himself, his, saw, to-him
sest	sat
sést	seen
سið	traditions
síðan	after, afterwards, since
síðasta	last
síður	less
sig	him
sigldu	sailed
sína	himself, his
sinn	his, theirs
sinna	his
sinnar	his
sinni	himself, his
síns	his
sínu	his
sínum	his
sitt	his
sjá	saw, see
sjálfráða	ourselves-decide
skaða	damage
skaði	harm
skal	shall
skáld	a-poet, poet
skálda	of-poets
skaldi	the-poet
skáldskap	poetry
skáldskapinn	poetry
skalt	shall
skaltu	shall, shall-you
skammar	shame
skapaðir	shaped
skegg	beard

Word List (Old Icelandic to English)

Old Icelandic	English	Old Icelandic	English
Skeggi	Skeggi (name)	*stafkarls*	as-a-beggar, beggar's
Skeggja	Skeggi (name)	*stafni*	staves
skildu	parted	*standa*	stand, stood
skip	a-ship, ship	*stef*	stave
skipaði	arranged	*stendur*	stood
skipi	ship	*steyptist*	disappeared
skipið	the-ship	*stóð*	stood
skips	ship, ships	*stóra*	large
skipti	exchanged	*stórættaður*	great-family
skjóta	launched	*stórauðigs*	great-wealth
skógum	forests, Skogar (place)	*stórfé*	great-wealth
skörulega	boldly	*stórmenni*	great-men
skörungur	noble	*strigadúk*	sack-cloth
skruma	show-off, swagger	*stumrar*	stumbled
skyldi	should	*stund*	awhile
skyldu	should	*stundlegum*	temporary
skyldur	should	*stutt*	short
slægða	slyness	*styrk*	support
sléttri	levelled	*suður*	south
slíkt	such	*sumar*	summer
smánar	humiliation	*sumir*	some
smíða	created	*sumrinu*	the-summer
snaraði	twisted	*svaf*	slept
snemma	early-age	*svara*	answered
snýr	turned	*svarar*	answered
snýst	turned	*Svarfaðardal*	Svarfardal (place)
sofnar	slept	*Svarfdæla*	Svarfardal (place)
sögðu	said	*svarri*	grave
sögu	saga	*Sveins*	Svein (name)
sögur	sagas	*svengd*	hungry
sölur	sale	*sverð*	a-sword
sömu	same	*sverðinu*	the-sword
son	son	*Svíþjóð*	Sweden (place)
sonar	son	*svo*	so
sótt	sought	*svöngum*	hunger
spurði	asked, learned	*sýnast*	appear
spurn	learned	*sýndist*	seemed-to
spurt	learned	*sýnduð*	give-performance
spyr	asked, asks, learned	*syni*	sons
spyrja	ask	*Syrgisdölum*	Syrgsdalir (place)
staðið	stand	*systra*	sisters
stafina	sticks	*systur*	sister
stafkarl	beggar		
stafkarla	beggars		
stafkarlar	beggars		

Word List (Old Icelandic to English)

Old Icelandic	English

T, t

Old Icelandic	English
taka	take, taken, took
talað	told
talar	said
tekið	taken
tekur	take, took
tíðinda	news
tíðindi	news
tíðindum	news
til	for, the, to, until
tíma	time
tímir	time
togar	pulled
tók	received, took
töluðu	told
trautt	scarcely
trémann	wooden-man
tröllskap	witchcraft
tunguna	tongue
tvær	two
tvo	two

Þ, þ

Old Icelandic	English
þá	then
það	it, that, the, this, with
þakkaði	thanked
þann	than, that, then
þar	them, there
þarf	needed
þarfa	needed
þarfaði	needed
þarfast	need
þarftu	need
þau	they
þegar	straightaway, there
þeim	them, then, they
þeir	they
þeirra	theirs, there
þeirrar	there
þengils	the-prince
þenna	the, then, these, this, those
þér	to-you, you
þess	this
þessa	this
þessar	this
þessi	this
þessu	this
þessum	this
þetta	this
þig	you
þín	your
þingi	assembly
Þingvelli	Thingvellir (place)
þinn	you
þinna	yours
þinni	yours
þínum	yours
þitt	yours
þjóanna	thighs
þjóðskáld	skilled-poet
þjóin	thighs
þjónustumenn	servants
Þjórsá	Thjorsa (place)
þó	though
þökk	thanks
þoku	fog
Þokuvísur	Fog-verses (name)
þola	endure
þoldu	endured
Þórðar	Thord (name)
Þorgarð	Thorgard (name)
Þorgarði	Thorgard (name)
Þorgarðs	Thorgard (name)
Þorgarður	Thorgard (name)
Þorgerði	Thorgerd (name)
Þórhildur	Thorhild (name)
Þorkell	Thorkell (name)
Þorleif	Thorleif (name)
Þorleifi	Thorleif (name), thorleif's
Þorleifr	Thorleif (name)
þorleifs	thorleif's, Thorleif's (name)
Þorleifur	Thorleif (name), Thorleif (name)
þorpara	peasant
þorsta	thirsty

Word List (Old Icelandic to English)

Old Icelandic	English
þótti	thought
þóttist	thought
þóttu	thought
þóttust	thought
Þrænda	the-Tronds' (name)
Þrándheim	Trondheim (place)
Þrasa	Thrasi (name)
þriðjung	third
þrjá	three
þrotnum	waning
þú	you
þunga	heavy
þurfa	need
því	accordingly, because, since, such, then, therefore
þvílíkri	accordingly-like
þykir	seems, thought
þykist	thought
þykjast	considered
þykklega	arrogantly

U, u

Old Icelandic	English
um	about, at
umráða	about-advice
undan	back, out-of
undarlega	strange
undir	under, up-to
ungum	young
unni	loved
upp	up, upped
upphaf	beginning
uppi	up
urðu	became
utan	out, without
utarlega	out-lying

Ú, ú

Old Icelandic	English
úr	from, from-out-of, of, out, out-of
úrigur	unruly
út	out, out-from
útferð	funeral
úti	finished, out
útlægur	outlaw
útlendis	other-lands

V, v

Old Icelandic	English
vænna	good
væri	was, were
vaknar	awake, awoke
vald	power
valdi	controlled
valdið	caused
vanda	care
vandist	did
vandræði	difficulty
vanur	experienced
var	was, were
varð	became, was, were
varla	scarcely
varning	wares
varninginn	wares
varpar	threw
vegsummerki	evidence, traces
veit	knows
veittu	granted
vel	well
veldur	brought-about
velli	the-fields
vellstæri	well-sized
vér	we
vera	be, becoming, being, be-it, to-be
verð	price
verða	become
verði	become, becomes
verðir	will-be
verðugu	honour
verðum	worth
verður	became, become
verið	became, been, made
verki	work
verr	worst
vert	had-been
vesaldar	wretchedness

Word List (Old Icelandic to English)

Old Icelandic	English	*Old Icelandic*	English
vestan	from-the-west, west	**Y, y**	
vestra	west		
vestur	west	yðrum	yours
vetra	winters	yður	you, yours
vetur	winter	yfir	over
veturinn	winter	yfirlæti	favour
vexti	grown	yngsti	youngest
við	by, from, to, with	Yngvildi	Yngvild (name)
víða	widely	ynni	win-over
viðskiptis	behaved	yrði	became
vígdjarfr	slaying-warrior	yrkja	compose
Vík	Vik (place)	ytra	outside
víkinni	the-bay		
vil	wish	**Ý, ý**	
vildi	wish, wished		
vildir	wish	ýmist	either
viljið	will	ýtar	out
viljum	wish, wish-to		
villumaðr	villain		
víls	advantage		
vinsæl	popular		
vinsældum	popularity		
virðingamaður	man-of-high-rank		
virðingar	honour		
virðum	worthiness		
visku	wisdom		
víst	know		
vísu	certainly, this-verse, verse		
vísuna	verse		
vísur	verses		
vita	certainly, knew, know		
vitja	know		
vitur	wise		
vó	killed		
völdum	doing		
völubrjótur	knuckle-breaker		
von	hope		
vonda	wicked		
vor	spring		
vordögum	spring-days		
vori	the-spring		
vorið	spring		
vort	ours		
voru	was, were		

Word List *(English to Old Icelandic)*

English	Old Icelandic
A, a	
a	að, eina, einn
about	á, að, í, um
about-advice	umráða
abuse	níð
accomplished-man	atgervimaður
accordingly	því
accordingly-like	þvílíkri
actually	reyndar
advantage	víls
adventure	ævintýr
advice	ráðum
after	áðr, aftur, eftir, síðan
after-the-case	eftirmáls
afterwards	eftir, síðan
age	aldri, aldur, elli, ellina
a-great	mikils
a-halberd	atgeir
a-little	lítillæti
all	alla, alla, allan, allir, allri, alls, allt, allt, öllu, öllum
all-great	allmikill
allow	láta
also	og
am	er
am-able	nýtan
a-man	maður
a-mark	mörk
amnesia	óminnis
ancestors	ætt
ancestry	ætt
ancient	fornum
ancient-ways	fornfræði, fornlegum
and	að, en, enda, og
angry	æfur
another	annar
another's	annars
answered	svara, svarar
any	nokkuð
anything	nokkur
a-poet	skáld
appear	sýnast
are	er, eru
are-you	ertu
a-ring	hring
arranged	skipaði
arrogantly	þykklega
art	listar
as	að, en, er, sem
as-a-beggar	stafkarls
a-second	annan
Asgeir (name)	Ásgeir, Ásgeiri
a-ship	skip
ask	spyrja
asked	bað, beiddi, beiddist, biður, spurði, spyr
asks	spyr
assembly	alþingi, þingi
assistance	ásjá, fulltingi
a-sword	sverð
at	á, að, í, um
ate	æti
Aud (name)	Auður, Auður
autumn	haustið
avenge	hefna
awake	vaknar
away	brot, brott, burt
awhile	hríð, stund
a-wife	koru
awoke	vaknar
a-woman	kora
B, b	
back	aftur, undan
back-driven	afturreka
bad	illa, illur
badly	illa
bag	hít
banquet	samsætis
bargaining	kaupslagar
battle-fire	gunnelds

Word List (English to Old Icelandic)

English	Old Icelandic
be	vera
beard	skegg
became	urðu, varð, verður, verið, yrði
because	því
become	orðið, verða, verði, verður
becomes	verði
becoming	gerist, vera
been	verið
before	áður, fyr, fyrir, fyrr
before him	fyrir
began	byrjaði, hóf
beggar	stafkarl
beggars	stafkarla, stafkarlar
beggar's	stafkarls
begin	hefja
beginning	upphaf
behaved	viðskiptis
being	sé, vera
be-it	vera
belonged	átt
belongings	góss
bench-fellows	bekkjunauta
better	batna, betur
bettered	batnaði
between	milli
bid	bað
blessed-life	sællífi
blizzard	él
Blonduos (place)	Blönduósi
boats	báts
body	búkinn, líkama
boldly	skörulega
booth	búð, búðar
booths	búðanna
both	báðir, bæði
bought	kaupir, keypti
bound	binda, bindur
bowels	iðrin
brave	frækni
break	brjótast
Brekka (place)	Brekku
bright	bjart
bring	færa
broad-waist	miðdigur
brother	bróður
brothers	bræðrum, bræður
brought	færa, færðu
brought-about	veldur
buried	heygður
burned	brenna, brenndu
burnt	brenna
but	en, enn, og
by	við

C, c

English	Old Icelandic
call	heita, kalla
called	heitir, kalla, kallaður, kölluðu
call-to	kalla
came	kemur, kom, koma, kominn, komst, komu
can	fæ, getur, kann
capable	gildur
care	gáir, vanda
cared	gáði
carried	báru, borið, bornir, færir
cast	kastaði
cattle	fé
caught	fengið, náði
caused	valdið
causing	framleiðslu
certainly	vísu, vita
character	gervi
chieftain	goði
chieftain-like	óhöfðinglegt
chieftains	höfðingja, höfðingjum
chieftains'	höfðingja
cleared	ræsta, ryðja, ryður
clearly	glögglega
close	fast, nálægt
closed	fast, lýkst
closely	fast
clothing	föt
coals	kolum
cold	köld, köldu, köldum
cold-bloodedly	kaldyrðum
combs	kömbum

Word List (English to Old Icelandic)

English	*Old Icelandic*	*English*	*Old Icelandic*
come	kom, koma, komast	destitution	andvana
comes	kemur, komi, kominn	devil's	fjandans
come-with	koma	devious	krókóttum
comfortable	hægt	did	gerði, gerðu, vandist
coming	kominn	died	andaður
commotion	háreysti	difficulty	vandræði
companions	félaga, förunauta	disappeared	hvarf, steyptist
compose	yrkja	disguise	gervina
considered	þykjast	disturbances	óspekt
controlled	valdi	doing	völdum
could	gæti, gat, kom	done	búið, gera, gert
courageous-warrior	hildardjarfi	doors	dyrum
craft	iðn	down	niður
created	smíða	dragon	naðrbings
crew	áhöfn, hásetum	draw	bregða
crutches	hækjur	drawn	dregur
cunning	kyndugskap	draws	dregr
cursed	bölvaðra	drew	draga, hrukku
custom	háttum	drift-wood	rekabút
customers	kaupunauta, kaupunautar	drink	drykkju
		drinking-tables	drykkjuborð
		drive	reka
		drowned	drekktur
		dungeon	dýflissu

D, d

damage	skaða
dark	dökkri, myrkt
daughter	dóttir
day	dag
days	dögum
dead	bani, dauðu
dearest	dýrstum
death	andlát
decayed	rotnað
deceived	blekkir
decreased	minnkaði
decrepitude	örverpi
deeds	atgervi
deem	dæmt
delegates	fulltrúa
Denmark (place)	Danmerkur
descended	kynjaður
descendents	ætt
desire	fýsi
desired	fýstist
desperation	örvænt

E, e

each	hverg, hverjum, hverri, hvert, hvorri
earl	jarl, jarli
Earl-Of-Lade (name)	Hlaðajarl, Hlaðajarls
earls	jarls
earl's-abuse	jarlsníðs
Earl's-Poet (name)	Jarlaskáld
early-age	snemma
east	austur
eat	át, eta
eighteen	átján
either	eða, ýmist
either-way	annaðhvort
eldest	elsti
elephant	fíl
end	enda, lokið
ends	lýkur
endure	þola

Word List (English to Old Icelandic)

English	Old Icelandic
endured	þoldu
England (place)	Englandi
enslavement	ánauð
equally	jafnan
equipped	gyrti
equipped-with	gyrður
Erik's (name)	Eiríks
errand	erindis
estate	óðali
evening	kveldið
events	atburð, atburðir
evidence	vegsummerki
evil	illu
evil-like	illslegur
exceedingly-much	geysimjög
excellent-man	íþróttamaður
except	nema
exchanged	skipti
experienced	vanur
Eyjafjoll-Mountains (place)	Eyjafjöllum

F, f

English	Old Icelandic
fair	sæmilega
Fair-Cheek (name)	Fagurkinn
fair-wind	byrjar
fame	frægt, orðstír
farm	búi
farmer	bónda
father	faðir, föður
favour	yfirlæti
fee-lot	fjárhlut
fell	féll, féllu, fellur
financial-loss	fjártjón
financial-share	fjárhlut
find	fund
finished	úti
first	fyrst
first-mate	háseta
fog	þoku
Fog-verses (name)	Þokuvísur
followed	fylgdi, fylgt
following	afliðið
following-men	fjölmenni

English	Old Icelandic
food	góða, kost, leiðarnests, matar
for	á, að, fyrir, í, til
forests	skógum
for-good	alfari
for-himself	sér
for-long	lengur
for-the-sake	sakir
forty	fertuga
forward	fram
foster-care	ástfóstur
fostered	fóstri
foster-father	fóstra
found	fann, finnur
from	á, að, af, af, er, frá, fram, í, úr, við
from-out-of	úr
from-the-west	vestan
from-told	frásagnar
full	fullu
full-coming	fullkomið
funeral	útferð

G, g

English	Old Icelandic
Gaseyri (place)	Gáseyri
gave	gaf, gáfu
generosity	örleik
get	fá, fæ, fást, geta, getur
ghastly	ljótu
gifted	lánað
gifts	gjafir
give	gefa
give-performance	sýnduð
gladly	gjarna
go	ganga
goat-beard	geitarskegg, geitarskegginu
God (name)	Guðs
going	farið, gengur
gone	farið, gengið
good	góðan, góðar, góðu, gott, vænna
got	fékk, fengi, fengið, gæti, gat, gekk

Word List (English to Old Icelandic)

English	Old Icelandic	English	Old Icelandic
got-married	kvæntist	heart	hjartað, hugr
granted	veittu	heaven's	himins
grave	svarri	heavy	þunga
great	mikill	he-had	honum
great-family	stórættaður	he-himself	sér
great-men	stórmenni	Hel (place)	Heju
great-wealth	stórauðigs, stórfé	held	hélt
greeted	kvaddi	Helgi (name)	Heg
greeting	kvaðningar	hellish-old-man	heljarkarl
grips	festist	here	hér, hingað
grown	vexti	hers	hennar
		high	hátt
		high-born	ítri
		him	hann, honum, sér, sig
		himself	sé, sér, sína, sinni
		hired	ræður
		his	hans, hánum, hins, honum, sér, sína, sinn, sinna, sinnar, sinni, síns, sínu, sínum, sitt

H, h

English	Old Icelandic
had	á, æti, átt, áttu, hafa, hafði, hefir, hefur, lætur, lagði, láta, láti, lét
had-been	vert
had-done	gerði
hair	hárið
Hakon (name)	Hákon, Hákonar
Hakon's (name)	Hákonar
halberd	atgeirnum
half	hálf
Hali (name)	Hali
Hallbjorn (name)	Hallbirni, Hallbjörn
hands	hendi
hanged	hengja
happened	gerðist
hardly	harðla
harm	skaði
harmful	dálegra
harsher	harðúðigur
has	er, hefir
hated	hataður
have	fá, hafa, hafi, hafið, haft, hefi, hefir, höfum, lagið
having	hefir
he	hann, hans, honum, sér
head-skin	höfuðsvörðum
hear	heyrið
heard	heyrði, heyrðu, heyrt

English	Old Icelandic
Hofdabrekka (place)	Höfðabrekku
hold	halda
home	heim
homes	heim
honour	sæmd, verðugu, virðingar
hope	von
Horgabrudi (name)	Hörgabrúði
Horgi (place)	Hörgi
however	hversu
how-so	hversu
humiliation	smánar
humility	lítillæti
hunger	svöngum
hungry	svengd

I, i

English	Old Icelandic
i	eg
i-am	mér
Iceland (place)	Ísland, Íslandi, Íslands
idol-worship	guðníðingskapur
if	ef, eg
ill	illa, illur

Word List (English to Old Icelandic)

English	Old Icelandic
improvement	góðu
in	á, að, af, í, inn
increase	aukið
in-front-of	framan
inherited	erfðu
instruction	fræðum
intended	ætlaði
into	í
invited	bað, boðið
iron-weapon	járn
Irpu (name)	Irpu
is	er
is-said	segja
it	á, að, hana, hún, það
itching	kláði
it-is	er
its	hennar
it-was	gerði

J, j

English	Old Icelandic
journey	ferðum, leið
Jutland (place)	Jóta

K, k

English	Old Icelandic
Karl (name)	Karl
kennings	kenningar
kill	drepa
killed	vó
king's-gift	konungsnaut
kinsmen	frænda
kinsmen-origins	kynferði
Klaufi (name)	Klaufa
knew	kunni, vita
knots	knúta
know	kannt, víst, vita, vitja
known	kenndur
knows	veit
knuckle-breaker	völubrjótur

L, l

English	Old Icelandic
Lade (place)	Hlaðir, Hlöðum
laid	lagði, lagið, lét, liggur
land	land
lands	lands
large	mikill, stóra
last	síðasta
laughed	hlógu
launched	skjóta
law-assembly	lögréttu
lay	liggur
laying	legið
learned	spurði, spurn, spurt, spyr
leave	orlof
left	lætur
legislation	lagasetning
lengthen	lengja
less	síður
let	lát, látið, lét
levelled	sléttri
lies	liggr, liggur
life	líf
life-days	lífsdaga
lifetime	lífstíma
like	líkar
liked	líkaði
liking	geðjast
listen	hlýða
listen-to	hlýdduð
little	lítils, lítinn
lived	bjó
Ljotolf (name)	Ljótólfi, Ljótólfs, Ljótólfur
locks	lásum
long	lengi
longer	lengra, lengur
lord	herra
lordship	höfðingskap
loved	unni
luck	giftu

M, m

English	Old Icelandic
made	ger, gera, gerðu, verið
magic	fítonsanda

Word List (English to Old Icelandic)

English	*Old Icelandic*
magical-arts	göldrum
malice	grálega
malignance	meinlætum
malignancy	meinlætis
man	karli, maður, mann
man-evil	mannillska
man-of-high-rank	virðingamaður
man's	manna
manslaughter	mannalát
many	marga, margan, margir, margra, margri, mart, mörg, mörgum
many-known	margkunnandi
market-town	kaupstaðinn
marshes	mörkum
matter	mál
may	má, mátti, mega, megi
me	mér, mig
meet	fund
men	drengr, manna, manna, menn, mönnum
merchant-ships	knarrar
merry	ærnri
met	hitti
middle	miðjum, miðs
middle-of	miðju
Midfjord (place)	Miðfirði
Midfjorder-Skeggi (name)	Miðfjarðar-Skeggja
midwinter-evening	aðfangskveld
mile	mílu
mine	minn, mitt
misery	eymd
misliked	mislíkaði
miss	missa
moment	bili
money	peninga
more	fleira, meir, meira
more-convenient	hentugri
morning	morguninn
most	flestum, mest, mesta, mesti, mikið
mother	móður
mother's-brother	móðurbróður
mound	haug, haugur
mouth	munn
move	flyttu
moved	gangi
movement	bragði
much	margra, mikið, mikil, mikill, mikils, mikinn, mikla, miklar, miklum, mjög
must	mur
Myrdal-Valley (place)	Mýdal
mysterious-path	refilstiga

N, n

English	*Old Icelandic*
name	heiti, nafn, nafni
named	heita, heiti, heitir, hét
name-giving	nafnfesti
nature	eðli, náttúra
near	nær
nearest	næstir
need	þarfast, þarftu, þurfa
needed	þarf, þarfa, þarfaði
never	aldrei
news	tíðinda, tíðindi, tíðindum
next	næsta
Nidung (name)	Níðungur
night	nætur, nátt
nineteen	nítján
Njord (name)	Njörðr
noble	öðlings, skörungur
noble-woman	kvenskörungur
noise	hark
no-little	ólítið
none	engi, engr, önga
nor	né
north	norður
Norway (place)	Noreg, Noregs
not	eiga, eigi, ekki, öngu
not-further	áfram
not-lacking	óvant
now	nú

Word List (English to Old Icelandic)

English	Old Icelandic

O, o

English	Old Icelandic
Odin (name)	Gautr
of	á, að, af, af, í, og, úr
of-all	öllum
off	af
of-gold	gulls
of-Hakon	hákoni
of-poets	skálda
often	oft, oftar, oftlega
of-the-ship	knarrar
Olaf (name)	Ólafur
Olaf's (name)	Ólafs
old	gamall, gamla, gömlum
old-man	gamlir, karl
omens	frétt, fréttar
on	á
one	eina, einn
one's	hvern
only	einna
open	opnast
opening	gíman
or	eða, ella
other	aðrar, aðrir, annar, annarra, annarri, hinum, öðrum
other-lands	útlendis
others	aðrir, annarra, öðrum
ours	vort
ourselves-decide	sjálfráða
out	úr, út, utan, úti, ýtar
out-from	út
outlaw	útlægur
out-lying	utarlega
out-of	undan, úr
outside	ytra
over	ofan, yfir
own	eigið
owning	eign
Oxara (place)	Öxará

P, p

English	Old Icelandic
parted	skildu
parting	reikar
passage	farning
passed	leið
peasant	þorpara
people	manna, manni, manninn, menn, mönnum
peoples'	mönnum
performed	flutt
pernickety	nákvæmi
phrases	drápu
plates	diska
plunder	férán
plundering	hervirki
poem	kvæði, kvæðið, kveðið
poems	kvæði
poem's-reward	kvæðislaunum
poet	skáld
poetry	brag, skáldskap, skáldskapinn
poles	ásum
popular	vinsæl
popularity	vinsældum
possible	hægt
power	krafti, mögnuðu, vald
powerful	ríkur
praise	lof
praised	lofaði
praise-words	lofkvæði
prepared	bjó, búinn, býr
previous-deeds	framaverka
price	verð
profit	græddi
promise	heita
promised	hét
promising	efnilegir
promptly	greiðlega
properly	sæmilega
proverb	orðskvið
provide	kost
provided-knowing	naddveiti
pulled	togar
punishment-time	hegningartíminn
put-to-words	kveðið

Word List (English to Old Icelandic)

English	Old Icelandic
Q, q	
quickly	bráðlega, greiðlega
R, r	
ran	hleypur
rather	heldur
received	tók
recently	litlu
recites	kveða
recovered	raknaði
Red (name)	Rauði
Red-Cloak (name)	Rauðfeldur
reddened	roðið
relief	létti
relieved	fegins
renown	hróðr
repaid	galt
repay	gjalda, launað
repayment	gjöld
reported	fréttust
requirements	hentar
rest	hvílast
restlessness	óværa, óværi
return	áður
returned	aftur
returning	aftur
revenge	hefnda
Reykir (place)	Reykjum
river	á
robbed	rændi
robbery	ránum
rocks	grjóti
rose	ríða, rís
rough	harðleikinn
ruled	réð
S, s	
sack-cloth	strigadúk
sacrifices	fórnir
saga	sögu
sagas	sögur
said	kvað, kveður, mælt, sagði, sagði, sagður, sagt, segið, segir, segja, sögðu, talar
sailed	sigldu
sake	sækja, sakir
sale	sölur
same	sömu
sand	eyri
sat	sat, sest
saw	sá, sér, sjá
say	kveða, segist, segja
say-you	segðu
scarcely	trautt, varla
scratched	hrífa
sea	haf
secrecy	laun
see	sé, sjá
seemed-to	sýndist
seems	þykir
seen	sést
sent	sendu
servants	þjónustumenn
settled	bjó, búið
settlement	byggða
shall	mun, munt, munuð, munum, skal, skalt, skaltu
shall-i	mig
shall-you	skaltu
shame	blygðar, skammar
shamed	forsmáður
shaped	skapaðir
she	hún
shepherd	sauðamaður
ship	skip, skipi, skips
ships	skips
shivering	hrollir
short	stutt
should	mun, munuð, skyldi, skyldu, skyldur
shoulders	herðar
show-off	skruma
shut	luktum

Word List (English to Old Icelandic)

English	Old Icelandic
side	megin
since	síðan, því
sister	systur
sisters	systra
sit	sæti, sætis
sit-still	kyrr
Skeggi (name)	Skeggi, Skeggja
skilled	íþrótt, íþróttir
skilled-in-magic	fjölkunni
skilled-poet	þjóðskáld
skills	íþrótta
Skogar (place)	Skógum
slaying-warrior	vígdjarfr
slendered	grenndi
slept	sofnar, svaf
slyness	slægða
so	sá, svo
soles-of-the-feet	iljarnar
solve	leysa
some	nokkuð, nokkura, nokkurar, nokkurt, sumir
something	nokkuð
somewhat	nokkuð
son	son, sonar
songs	atkvæðum
son-of-gjallandi	gjallandason
sons	syni
soon	fljótlega
soonest	fljótasta
sorcery	galdur
sought	fréttist, leitaði, sótt
soul	andar
south	suður
speak	kveða
spikes	broddur
spoke	kvað, mælti
spoken	kveðið
spring	vor, vorið
spring-days	vordögum
stand	staðið, standa
stave	stef
staves	stafni
sticks	stafina
stood	standa, stendur, stóð
stopped	linnir
stories	saga
straightaway	þegar
strange	kynstrum, undarlega
strangeness	býsn
strong	gilds
struck	hjó
stumbled	stumrar
such	slíkt, því
summer	sumar
support	styrk
supposed	ætluðu
Svarfardal (place)	Svarfaðardal, Svarfdæla
Svein (name)	Sveins
swagger	skruma
Sweden (place)	Svíþjóð
swords	branda
Syrgsdalir (place)	Syrgisdölum

T, t

English	Old Icelandic
take	náms, numið, taka, tekur
taken	nema, taka, tekið
talented	gervilegur
talked	mælti
teach	kenna
temple	hofi
temples	hof
temporary	stundlegum
than	en, þann
thanked	þakkaði
thanks	þökk
that	á, að, en, er, sem, það, þann
the	að, en, er, hið, hinn, hinni, hins, hinu, það, þenna, til
the-abuse	níðið
the-bag	hítina
the-bay	víkinni
the-best	mest, mesta
the-chieftain	goða
the-coals	kol
the-crutches	hækjurnar

Word List (English to Old Icelandic)

English	Old Icelandic	*English*	Old Icelandic
the-darkness	myrkrið	thick-clouds	mökkr
the-day	daginn	thighs	þjóanna, þjóin
the-earl	jarl, jarli, jarlinn, jarlinum, jarls	Thingvellir (place)	Þingvelli
		think	hugsa
the-earl's	jarls	third	þriðjung
the-earl's-abuse	jarlsníði	thirsty	þorsta
the-earth	jörðina	this	á, að, það, þenna, þess, þessa, þessar, þessi, þessu, þessum, þetta
the-enemy's	óvinarins		
the-fellows	drengjum		
the-fields	velli		
the-greatest	mestr	this-verse	vísu
the-hall	höllina, höllinni	Thjorsa (place)	Þjórsá
theirs	sinn, þeirra	Thord (name)	Þórðar
the-king	konung, konungi, konungs, konungur	Thorgard (name)	Þorgarð, Þorgarði, Þorgarðs, Þorgarður
the-land	land, landi	Thorgerd (name)	Þorgerði
the-lion's	leóns	Thorhild (name)	Þórhildur
them	þar, þeim	Thorkell (name)	Þorkell
the-mauler	böggva	Thorleif (name)	Þorleif, Þorleifi, Þorleifr, Þorleifur, Þorleifur
the-most	flestu		
the-mound	hauginn, hauginum, haugurinn		
		thorleif's	þorleifi, þorleifs
the-mound-dweller	haugbúann	Thorleif's (name)	Þorleifs
then	að, en, hið, hina, þá, þann, þeim, þenna, því	those	hinn, þenna
		though	þó
		thought	þótti, þóttist, þóttu, þóttust, þykir, þykist
the-night	nóttina		
the-old-man	karl, karli	thoughts	hug
the-poem	kvæðið	Thrasi (name)	Þrasa
the-poet	skaldi	three	þrjá
the-prince	þengils	threw	varpar
there	þar, þegar, þeirra, þeirrar	through	gegnum
		tied-up	binda
therefore	því	time	tíma, tímir
the-same	samur	to	á, að, í, til, við
these	þenna	to-be	vera
the-ship	nökkvi, skipið	to-carry	flytja
the-spring	vori	to-eat	etið
the-straw	hálminn	together	saman
the-summer	sumrinu	to-give	gefa
the-sword	sverðinu	to-hear	hlýða
the-tables	borð	to-him	honum, sér
the-Tronds' (name)	Þrænda	told	sagði, talað, töluðu
the-uppermost	ofanverðum	told-of	getið
they	þau, þeim, þeir	to-me	mér
they-were	eru	tongue	tunguna

Word List (English to Old Icelandic)

English	Old Icelandic
took	nam, taka, tekur, tók
torment	kvala
to-sell	selja
tough	seigt
toughness	harðfengi
to-you	þér
traces	vegsummerki
trading-men	kaupmönnum
traditions	sið
transport	reiða
travel	fara, ferð, ferðar
travel-goods	fararefna
travelled	farið, fer, fór, fóru
tricked	bregður, ginnti
Trondheim (place)	Þrándheim
troubled	bæginn
truly	sannlega
tunic	kyrtilinn, kyrtlinum
turned	hverfur, snýr, snýst
twisted	snaraði
two	tvær, tvo
true	satt

U, u

English	Old Icelandic
unconsciousness	óvit
under	undir
undone	ógert, óloknum
un-eagerly	ófreklegar
un-glad	ógleður
un-gladdened	ógladdist
un-gladness	ógleði
unknown	ókunna
unless	nema
un-redeemable	óbætilegs
unruly	úrigur
unsoundly	óhljóði
until	til
up	upp, uppi
upped	upp
upper	efsta
up-to	undir
us	oss
usually	jafnan

V, v

English	Old Icelandic
vacations	orlofs
verse	vísu, vísuna
verses	vísur
Vik (place)	Vík
villain	villumaðr
vocabulary	orðfæri

W, w

English	Old Icelandic
walked	gekk
waning	þrotnum
wares	varning, varninginn
warrior	gramr
warriors	fyrðum
was	enn, er, væri, var, varð, voru
was-named	hét, nefndist
wave	öldu
we	oss, vér
wealth	fé
wealth-damage	fjárskaða
wealthy	auðigur
we-are	eru
well	vel
well-sized	vellstæri
went	fékk, fer, fór, fóru, ganga,ганganda, gekk, gengur
were	væri, var, varð, voru
west	vestan, vestra, vestur
what	er, hvað, sem
wheel	röðla
when	en, er
whether	hvort
which	er, sem
who	er, hver
who's	hverjum
who-was	er
why	hví
wicked	vonda
widely	víða
wife	kona

Word List (English to Old Icelandic)

English	Old Icelandic
will	viljið
will-be	verðir
willingly	ofléttlega
win-over	ynni
winter	vetur, veturinn
winters	vetra
wisdom	visku
wise	vitur
wish	vil, vildi, vildir, viljum
wished	vildi
wish-to	viljum
witchcraft	fjölkynngi, gerningum, tröllskap
with	í, með, það, við
with-conviction	sakir
without	án, utan
woman	kona
Woman-Verses (name)	Konurvísur
wooden-man	trémann
worded	ort
words	orð, orðið, ort, orti
work	verki
worst	verr
worth	verðum
worthiness	virðum
would	mundi, mundu
wretchedness	vesaldar
written	rituð

Y, y

Yngvild (name)	Yngvildi
you	þér, þig, þinn, þú, yður
young	ungum
youngest	yngsti
your	þín
yours	þinna, þinni, þínum, þitt, yðrum, yður
Yule (name)	Jóla
yule-feast	jólaveislunnar

A Word Comparison of Old Norse and Old Icelandic Words

Old Norse	Old Icelandic	English
áðr	áður	before
áðr	áður	return
aftr	aftur	after
aftr	aftur	back
aftr	aftur	returned
aftr	aftur	returning
aldr	aldur	age
andaðr	andaður	died
ástfóstr	ástfóstur	foster-care
at	að	a
at	að	about
at	að	and
at	að	as
at	að	at
at	að	for
at	að	from
at	að	in
at	að	it
at	að	of
at	að	that
at	að	the
at	að	then
at	að	this
at	að	to
atgervimaðr	atgervimaður	accomplished-man
atkvœðum	atkvæðum	songs
auðigr	auðigur	wealthy
Auðr	Auður	Aud (name)
austr	austur	east
bat	bað	asked
bat	bað	bid
bat	bað	invited
betr	betur	better
biðr	biður	asked
bindr	bindur	bound
bœði	bæði	both
bœginn	bæginn	troubled
bregðr	bregður	tricked
broddr	broddur	spikes
bróðr	bróður	brother
brœðr	bræður	brothers
brœðrum	bræðrum	brothers
Danmerkr	Danmerkur	Denmark (place)
dœmt	dæmt	deem
dregr	dregur	drawn
drekktr	drekktur	drowned
fellr	fellur	fell
finnr	finnur	found
föðr	föður	father
fœ	fæ	can
fœ	fæ	get
fœra	færa	bring
fœra	færa	brought
fœrðu	færðu	brought
fœrir	færir	carried
fornfrœði	fornfræði	ancient-ways
forsmáðr	forsmáður	shamed
frœðum	fræðum	instruction
frœgt	frægt	fame
frœkni	frækni	brave
frœnda	frænda	kinsmen
galdr	galdur	sorcery
gengr	gengur	going
gengr	gengur	went
gervilegr	gervilegur	talented
getr	getur	can
getr	getur	get
geysimjǫk	geysimjög	exceedingly-much
gildr	gildur	capable
gœti	gæti	could
gœti	gæti	got
grœddi	græddi	profit
guðníðingskapr	guðníðingskapur	idol-worship
gyrðr	gyrður	equipped-with

A Word Comparison of Old Norse and Old Icelandic

Old Norse	Old Icelandic	English	Old Norse	Old Icelandic	English
harðúðigr	harðúðigur	harsher	liggr	liggur	laid
hataðr	hataður	hated	liggr	liggur	lay
haugr	haugur	mound	liggr	liggur	lies
hefr	hefur	had	lítillœti	lítillæti	a-little
heldr	heldur	rather	lítillœti	lítillæti	humility
heygðr	heygður	buried	Ljótólfr	Ljótólfur	Ljotolf (name)
hingat	hingað	here	lœtr	lætur	had
hjartat	hjartað	heart	lœtr	lætur	left
hleypr	hleypur	ran	lofkvœði	lofkvæði	praise-words
hœgt	hægt	comfortable	lýkr	lýkur	ends
hœgt	hægt	possible	maðr	maður	a-man
hœkjr	hækjur	crutches	maðr	maður	man
hœkjurnar	hækjurnar	the-crutches	meinlœtis	meinlætis	malignancy
hvat	hvað	what	meinlœtum	meinlætum	malignance
hverfr	hverfur	turned	miðdigr	miðdigur	broad-waist
illr	illur	bad	mjǫk	mjög	much
illr	illur	ill	móðr	móður	mother
illslegr	illslegur	evil-like	móðrbróðr	móðurbróður	mother's-brother
íþróttamaðr	íþróttamaður	excellent-man	mœlt	mælt	said
kallaðr	kallaður	called	mœlti	mælti	spoke
kemr	kemur	came	mœlti	mælti	talked
kemr	kemur	comes	nákvœmi	nákvæmi	pernickety
kenndr	kenndur	known	nálœgt	nálægt	close
Konrvísr	Konurvísur	Woman-Verses (name)	niðr	niður	down
			Níðungr	Níðungur	Nidung (name)
konungr	konungur	the-king	nœr	nær	near
kvat	kvað	said	nœsta	næsta	next
kvat	kvað	spoke	nœstir	næstir	nearest
kveðr	kveður	said	nœtr	nætur	night
kvenskörungr	kvenskörungur	noble-woman	nokkr	nokkur	anything
kvœði	kvæði	poem	norðr	norður	north
kvœði	kvæði	poems	óbœtilegs	óbætilegs	un-redeemable
kvœðið	kvæðið	poem			
kvœðið	kvæðið	the-poem	œfr	æfur	angry
kvœðislaunum	kvæðislaunum	poem's-reward	œrnri	ærnri	merry
kvœntist	kvæntist	got-married	œti	æti	ate
kynjaðr	kynjaður	descended	œti	æti	had
lánat	lánað	gifted	œtlaði	ætlaði	intended
launat	launað	repay	œtluðu	ætluðu	supposed
lengr	lengur	for-long	œtt	ætt	ancestors
lengr	lengur	longer	œtt	ætt	ancestry
			œtt	ætt	descendents

A Word Comparison of Old Norse and Old Icelandic

Old Norse	Old Icelandic	English
ævintýr	ævintýr	adventure
ógleðr	ógleður	un-glad
Ólafr	Ólafur	Olaf (name)
orðfœri	orðfæri	vocabulary
örvœnt	örvænt	desperation
óvœra	óværa	restlessness
óvœri	óværi	restlessness
Rauðfeldr	Rauðfeldur	Red-Cloak (name)
ríkr	ríkur	powerful
rœðr	ræður	hired
rœndi	rændi	robbed
rœsta	ræsta	cleared
rotnat	rotnað	decayed
ryðr	ryður	cleared
sagðr	sagður	said
samr	samur	the-same
samsœtis	samsætis	banquet
sauðamaðr	sauðamaður	shepherd
síðr	síður	less
skörungr	skörungur	noble
skyldr	skyldur	should
slœgða	slægða	slyness
sœkja	sækja	sake
sœllífi	sællífi	blessed-life
sœmd	sæmd	honour
sœmilega	sæmilega	fair
sœmilega	sæmilega	properly
sœti	sæti	sit
sœtis	sætis	sit
sögr	sögur	sagas
sölr	sölur	sale
stendr	stendur	stood
stórœttaðr	stórættaður	great-family
suðr	suður	south
Svarfdœla	Svarfdæla	Svarfardal (place)
systr	systur	sister
talat	talað	told
tekr	tekur	take
tekr	tekur	took
þat	það	it
þat	það	that
þat	það	the
þat	það	this
þat	það	with
Þokuvísr	Þokuvísur	Fog-verses (name)
Þorgarðr	Þorgarður	Thorgard (name)
Þórhildr	Þórhildur	Thorhild (name)
Þorleifr	Þorleifur	Thorleif (name)
Þrœnda	Þrænda	the-Tronds' (name)
tvœr	tvær	two
úrigr	úrigur	unruly
útlœgr	útlægur	outlaw
vandrœði	vandræði	difficulty
vanr	vanur	experienced
veldr	veldur	brought-about
vellstœri	vellstæri	well-sized
verðr	verður	became
verðr	verður	become
vestr	vestur	west
vetr	vetur	winter
vinsœl	vinsæl	popular
vinsœldum	vinsældum	popularity
virðingamaðr	virðingamaður	man-of-high-rank
vísr	vísur	verses
vitr	vitur	wise
vœnna	vænna	good
vœri	væri	was
vœri	væri	were
völubrjótr	völubrjótur	knuckle-breaker
yðr	yður	you
yðr	yður	yours
yfirlœti	yfirlæti	favour